PRAISE FOR VALLEY LIFE

As human beings, we were designed to live in a garden paradise. But this world is no longer a garden or a paradise, and too often we find ourselves in the valley of despair. Yolanda Cohen Stith has journeyed into this valley. She has also experienced the love and grace of God so fully that she has had triumph in her tears. I heartily recommend *Valley Life*. May the Holy Spirit use it to lead you through the dark valley, to the light of His love and the feast He has prepared for you (Psalm 23).

Pastor Frank Friedmann
Grace Life Fellowship
Baton Rouge, LA

Yolanda Cohen Stith is one of the most amazing, resilient, authentic people I've ever met. I am honored and humbled to have watched Yolanda begin to slowly, humbly, and boldly embrace her journey through the valley following the death of her husband. Assuming you've picked up this book because you or someone you love is traveling through a valley, I encourage you to listen closely to Yolanda's story and share in her discoveries. She's been there and offers emotional guidance and spiritual perspective to all of us navigating pain and powerlessness.

Scott F. Heine, D. Min
Senior Pastor, Hope Christian Fellowship
Vint Hill, VA

When you walk into your valley of shadows, you will need a guide you can trust. Yolanda Stith is such a guide, as she has walked deep valleys. In *Valley Life* she provides a depth of perspective that comes only from those who have joined the fellowship of God's suffering.

David Lyons
The Navigators International Vice President
Coauthor of Don't Waste the Pain: Learning To Grow Through Suffering

Reading *Valley Life*, I was drawn into Yolanda's story immediately, where the important truths she conveys embraced me with power and comfort. If you'd like to know what God's work and grace looks and feels like through the traumas and joys of life, this is your book.

Ralph Harris
President of Ralph Harris Ministries
Pastor, speaker, and best-selling author of Life According to Perfect and God's Astounding Opinion of You

Yolanda gives us an uncommon gift. She tells on herself. *Valley Life* is not a cliched series of triumphant success stories with lectures on how to have a Christian testimony like hers. Yolanda is vulnerable. She takes us on an honest journey of grief, healing, and freedom. She models and explains grace. She replaces trying harder with learning to live out of who God says she is and who He is in her. Well done, friend.

John Lynch
Coauthor of The Cure *and author of* On My Worst Day

Valley Life is an authentic account of life in Christ through losses great and small. As a "Valley girl" from Southern California, Yolanda uses her unique experiences to help us cultivate an appreciation for life in the valley. She shows us that the valley is a place of "higher learning" rather than a place of punishment—and that ultimately it empowers us to access life in Christ as nothing else can.

Dr. Nicole Fitzpatrick
Licensed Psychologist
Director of Hyde Park Counseling

VALLEY LIFE

VALLEY LIFE

FINDING GOD IN THE MIDST OF YOUR PAIN

YOLANDA COHEN STITH

ILLUMIFY MEDIA GLOBAL
Littleton, Colorado

The views and opinions expressed in this book are those of the author and
do not necessarily reflect the official policy or position of Illumify Media
Global.

Unless otherwise specified all Scripture is from the NASB version.
Copyright © 1960, 1962, 1963, 1968, 1971, 1972, 1973, 1975, 1977, 1995 by
The Lockman Foundation. Scripture marked ESV is from the The Holy
Bible, English Standard Version. ESV® Text Edition: 2016. Copyright ©
2001 by Crossway Bibles, a publishing ministry of Good News Publishers.
Scripture marked MSG is from the Message, Copyright © 1993, 2002, 2018
by Eugene H. Peterson. Scripture marked KJV is from the King James
Version, which is in the public domain.

Published by
Illumify Media Global
www.IllumifyMedia.com
"Write. Publish. Market. *SELL!*"

Library of Congress Control Number: 2019916642

Paperback ISBN: 978-1-949021-82-0
eBook ISBN: 978-1-949021-83-7

Cover design by Debbie Lewis

Printed in the United States of America

To my late husband, Ken, who believed in me, encouraged me, and shared life with me
and
To the God of Abraham, Isaac, and Jacob who blessed me with Ken and Life in Messiah Jesus

TABLE OF CONTENTS

ACKNOWLEDGMENTS

This book would not be possible without the contributions of all the people in my life who have, in one way or another, provided practical help and those who have been key players in all the valleys I've walked through. I am most thankful for my late husband, Ken, my two children, Rachel and Benjamin and his wife, Jessica, my son by marriage, Saalik and his family; and my four grandchildren, Madelyn, Jacob, Sammy, and Catalina. Without you, I would not have grown up and become a responsible, loving, and caring individual.

I am most grateful to God for leading me to Grace Ministries, Inc. in Manassas, Virginia, where I discovered my identity as a child of God and the secret to Life in Jesus. It was through my personal counseling experience, training, and staff participation for seventeen years that my Bible knowledge was transformed into moment-by-moment living from the God I love.

There are many others to thank, as well. Pamela Sarver, president of Word Framer, my longtime friend and editor was invaluable to me and without her, I couldn't have produced my manuscript. Her attention to detail and flow was incredibly helpful. Margo Heine is my faithful friend and sister by faith, former colleague, editor for New Heart Living, partner in crime, and the one who introduced me to Fireball. Scott Heine, pastor at Hope Christian Fellowship in Vint Hill, Virginia, is not only a loyal friend and spiritual colleague, but a great listener and truth teller. Cindy Zobel, another one of my besties and sister by faith, is the president of my personal fan club and I hers, Board Member for New Heart Living, encourager, and shopping maven. Gil Eng drops everything when I have technical issues. My son in-law, Soon Moon, races at my beck and call when something in my house breaks or doesn't work and thinks I'm crazy but loves me anyway. And, of course, there are my New Heart Living followers and my Tres Dias family, including all those in North Georgia, Southern Ontario, as well as Northern Virginia; whom God has used to give me the confidence to write this book. You are my greatest cheerleaders, and I love you all!

PREFACE

Here I sit, recently widowed and trying to adjust to a catastrophic change in my life; a change I never imagined happening at a mere sixty-three years old. Sure, widowhood would likely come later, maybe when I am eighty or ninety, but not now when Ken and I both felt so young and our lives were so full. Of course, this is not the first time in my forty years of walking with God that I have experienced pain and heartache. But it was this loss of all losses which caused me to finally put pen to paper and share with you what I've learned in my journey through those valleys, implementing a lesson I've learned: when I'm in pain, use that pain as a catalyst to stimulate my creative energy. I've felt for some time that I had a story to tell—my story—that would hopefully inspire, encourage, and give hope to anyone who happened to read these pages.

Admittedly, this has been a stop and start venture for years, since I don't like rejection and I was never entirely certain that anyone would be remotely interested in what I had to say, certainly not a publisher. Could I handle the rejection if I don't get published? Well, it's taken me a while to choose to believe the truth: that my worth and value as a person—my identity—is not tied to what a publisher thinks or whether or not this book is read by more than a handful of people. My only desire is that my valley experiences— whether caused by the effects of living in a fallen world, the forces of evil, or the self-centeredness of others or my own —can be used to bless and enlighten someone else who has spent more than their fair share of time in the valley.

INTRODUCTION

You know you're a Valley Girl when your gender is female, you grew up in the San Fernando Valley in Los Angeles or you've spent a great deal of time as a follower of Messiah Jesus schlepping through the valleys of life. Okay, I admit it, I'm a Valley Girl. Guilty on all counts.

My San Fernando Valley beginnings notwithstanding, I am well acquainted with the valleys that come with living in a fallen world. Perhaps you are as well, and perhaps it's why you decided to pick up this book.

You know you're a Valley Girl if you've learned that the secret to Christian life is *in the valley*—in the places of struggle. My own valleys are what led me to God in the first place as a twenty-four year old Jewish girl raised to have nothing to do with Christianity. I desperately wanted peace and fulfillment and spiritual answers to my questions. Much to the horror of my parents, all roads led me to a Jewish Messiah who had, through my Jewish lens and perspective, been masquerading as a Gentile.

When God revealed Himself to me, my life radically

changed and I, a self-centered and irreverent hippie, became a brand new person with different motivations, desires, goals, and thoughts about life and eternal things. In essence, my life took a one eighty!

Like most novices, in the beginning of my journey with Messiah, I thought my life would be smooth sailing, that all my problems would be over, and as the saying goes (especially if you come from Hollywood where dreams are made), I would live happily ever after. But that didn't happen, of course. Instead, it was the valleys of my life that God used to teach me about the Christian life—His life in me—and about living *from* Him rather than *for* Him. It has been anything but smooth sailing, but I have never had a moment of regret or doubt, since the day I invited Jesus to be this Jewish girl's Messiah.

My journey includes some pretty magnificent mountain tops. but it's the valleys that have been most valuable in my life since they are the classrooms where I learn the truths that anchor my soul and motivate me to persevere in my darkest moments, even to the point of literally saving my life at one point. My valley experiences have shaped me and made me the person I am today, and they are preparing me for the things I will encounter tomorrow, not that I want to think about that at present!

The valleys of life are certainly not feel-good times of kicking up your heels and shouting "Yeehaw!" Far from it. You'll never find people lining up for valley duty by choice and if you do, well, they aren't in their right mind! In fact, whenever I see a valley off in the distant horizon coming into view, I begin to look for a quick detour, a safer route to take. Unfortunately, I've never really been successful at finding detours. God is always faithful to get me back on course from being diverted by the Adversary's tactic of fear and dread. The easy road, the road without obstacles and challenges, is fruitless. My valleys have been divinely appointed opportunities for my greatest growth, my class-room of higher learning, and my times of experiencing the power and presence of the resurrected Jesus within me. Valleys are the places where God is most glorified in the lives of His children.

God gives birth to kings in the valleys. Blind men receive sight and sighted men become blind in the valleys. Battles are fought and victories are won in the valleys. Giants and walls fall in the valleys. The real power of God is not experienced on the mountaintops, but in the valley when we are reminded that we are weak and helpless, and our strength can only be found in Him.

Fear, dread, anxiety, and depression are natural responses to valley experiences, unless we look for God's presence in the valley and believe the truth that He's always there with us. In the book of Hosea, God promises His people restoration and hope in the Valley of Achor. "Therefore, behold, I will allure her, bring her into the wilderness, and speak kindly to her. Then I will give her vineyards from there, and the Valley of Achor as a door of hope" (Hosea 2:14-15). The Valley of Achor is a reference from the book of Joshua. When Joshua and his army conquered the city of Jericho, Joshua told them that all the plunder was off-limits and must be set-aside for the Lord. Achan, however, stole and hid some of the plundered gold and silver to keep for himself. As a result, God allowed Israel to be defeated by the Amorites. When Achan's treachery was revealed, all of his possessions were taken and brought to the Valley of Achor and he and his family, as well as all that he owned were destroyed. After that, the Valley of Achor became known as the Valley of Trouble

(Joshua 7:26). Yet we see in the book of Hosea that God promises us a door of hope in the Valley of Trouble!

What was it that motivated Achan to take the plunder when he knew that it was to be designated for the Lord? The easy answer is that it was his greed. If so, what was it that motivated his greed? I believe it was fear. Perhaps Achan was afraid that he wouldn't have enough money to pay his mortgage, or he needed to upgrade to a newer model chariot to keep up with the Goldbergs. I don't know, but fear will always lead us to our fleshly ways of coping, and when we are afraid, we look for ways apart from God to *feel* secure.

We learn to fear the valleys in life and try desperately to avoid them because of the pain that we experience in them. But the Lord leads us to the valleys to challenge our fleshly ways of living, not because He wants to punish us, but because He wants us to experience the freedom that we can know through life found in Jesus; rather than the imitation of life found through man's efforts (his performance, human resources, and coping strategies).

Our fear of the valleys originates from the lies we have come to believe. The lies may be concerning God's faithfulness, His sovereignty, and our identity; all of which give way to fear. But the only way to deal with the fear is to experience Jesus as our security while we are there. The Evil One would have us believe that real security comes from avoiding painful circumstances, but that is not genuine security. It is merely a feeling produced by an illusion, a circumstance, which can change in a moment and often does.

I don't know about you, but if you're anything like me, you haven't been very successful in controlling your circumstances. Am I right? We can, however, control what we're going to believe *in* our circumstances, what we are going to believe about our security in Him, no matter what valley we face. The valleys in our lives can be the perfect places to produce the kind of fruit in us that truly satisfies our souls and glorifies Him. Through Jesus, God can turn the Valley of Trouble into a door of hope.

THE NIGHTMARE

There is no easy walk to freedom anywhere, and many of us will have to pass through the valley of the shadow of death again and again before we reach the mountaintop of our desires.

—Nelson Mandela

One thing is certain: everyone experiences loss in this world. For some, the loss is so devastating and life-altering that it leaves them motionless and mute. Even though loss and the pain that accompanies it are a natural by-product of living in a fallen world, the effects can be so traumatic and paralyzing that a person hardly knows how to move beyond it and find healing. It could be the loss of one's ability to function independently, the loneliness one might feel when a close friend moves far way, a tornado that blows through town and destroys your home, a marriage that falls apart like a once-beautiful crystal vase smashed to the ground into a million tiny shards of glass, or the death of your child or spouse. The list is endless, and the pain can be debilitating and blinding when it comes into your life like a tsunami and leaves wreckage everywhere; or like a thief in the middle of the night, robbing you of the security and comfort you had once enjoyed.

For the most part, there's no way to control what happens in life. Wherever we go and with whom, pain will find us because we live in a broken world with broken people. The pain we experience is the bucket of ice water thrown into our face to remind us of those little details. Pain propels us out of our comfort zone and hurdles us into a place of difficulty and challenge that we don't like and didn't invite, at least not intentionally. So when it comes and imposes itself upon us, what do we do? How do we cope? And more importantly, how do we fix it and can we? Those were my questions and perhaps yours too.

How did I get here? I ask myself this question frequently as I sit and rehearse the past four years in my mind. I had been married to a great guy for thirty-five years. I never imagined my life without him; I never had reason to. Well, okay, based on statistics and the fact that he had six years on me, he would, most likely, precede me in death, but who really thinks about that? Not me. In the same way, I never thought about earthquakes and uncontrollable fires when I lived in Southern California, but they happen.

In September 2014, it appeared that Ken and I were nearing the end of a painful ten-year valley experience with our twenty-five-year old son, Benjamin. He had decided he'd had enough of drugs and their inherent lifestyle and took us up on our offer to go to an inpatient treatment facility in Tennessee with the purpose of changing his life.

Ben poured himself into the program, attending all the therapies, getting involved with the Bible studies, and even playing guitar on the worship team. Consequently, the staff was very impressed. One thing I can say about my son is that whatever he does he does 100 percent, sort of like his mother.

A family weekend was scheduled at Ben's treatment facility in November of 2014. In the months leading up to that time, I began to notice some peculiarities with Ken—chronic headaches, complaints about tingling in his neck, poor driving, mental confusion, and memory loss. Even though I didn't dream these symptoms meant anything so serious as to be life-threating, I urged him to go to his doctor for a check-up. His doctor didn't do anything more than take his blood and vitals and found nothing alarming. At the time, I questioned this no further. After all, at sixty-six years of age, Ken was the picture of health, playing full court basketball with a bunch of young men and wiping up the floor with them—his words not mine!

It was at the family weekend in Tennessee, when Ken suddenly walked straight into a wall and his headaches became so severe he doubled over in pain, that I realized something was terribly wrong. Upon arriving back home, I took him straight to Bethesda Suburban Hospital where they did a CAT scan and then an MRI. He was promptly admitted to a private room. I don't think I had ever been in an emergency room as a walk-in and seen everything move so fast. I'm guessing that the symptoms I described, coupled with the CAT scan results, really got their attention. The neurologist on duty came in and said, "Mrs. Stith, your husband is in critical condition and needs immediate surgery. He has a very large brain tumor." Okay. I knew I wasn't going crazy. Here was the answer to all the strange occurrences and behaviors I had been seeing over a period of about three months. But I never expected to get this news. I immediately shifted into proactive high gear. When faced with a problem, I automatically begin to look for a way to solve it. Even though I'd known people who died from brain tumors, my mind would not let me go there. All my mind could contain was the initial impact of this very bad news. I couldn't think about what comes next week or next month. It was like I imagine an out-of-body experience; being faced with something beyond my comprehension and ability to cope. It was like watching a movie of myself in that situation.

We rushed Ken up to Johns Hopkins Hospital in Baltimore, about an hour away, so that he could be seen by one of the country's premier neurosurgeons—the benefit of Ken working at National Institutes of Health (NIH) and knowing all the right people. His doctor was the chief of neurosurgery and one of the best in his field. The only way one would be fortunate enough to get this doctor is if they were someone of notoriety or knew the right people. Ken was the latter. He was scheduled for a biopsy to make a positive diagnosis and determine treatment. At this point, I'm thinking positively and trusting the Lord to heal Ken because, after all, look at what we've already been through in our lives. Surely we've reached our quota for valley duty, right? We're going to get a break this time and God is going to heal Ken. When it comes to the supernatural, I'd always believed that God wasn't limited by the rules of nature. God is bigger than a freakin' tumor.

And what about my son back in Tennessee still working on his issues? God has to heal Ken or Benjamin will fall apart and go right back to the gutter or worse! If I were

God, I'd be looking at my options and thinking that a supernatural healing was in order.

When we were out in the waiting room with our friends, Margo and Scott, who had driven three hours to sit with my daughter Rachel and me, Ken's surgeon finally emerged from the biopsy surgery and escorted us into The Room. "Mrs. Stith," he said, "I'm sorry to tell you that our suspicions were correct. Your husband has a glioblastoma multiforme, level 4." I was thinking, *okay, that doesn't sound go*od, but I was clueless to know just how *not good* it was. He barely got his words out when, in the corner of my eye, I saw Rachel crumble to the floor sobbing. She knew about GBM's, because her close friend's father had died from one. I had never heard the term and was completely in the dark as the highly skilled, knowledgeable, and compassionate surgeon was determined to paint a rosy picture for us. Why do they do this? I don't want a rosy picture. I want the truth, even if the truth is hard to bear. They sent him home to await surgery to remove the beast. A GBM doubles in size every two weeks, which meant there was no time for delay or indecisiveness, neither of which could ever be attributed to me and how I roll.

We managed to celebrate Thanksgiving together before Ken went back up to Hopkins to have the tumor removed. A beast it proved to be. As it happens, they could only remove a portion of the tumor. Little did I know the effects brain surgery would have on him, even though I was given a huge stack of medical literature to read about it. Did they really expect me to read and understand all that medical terminology and legal jargon in the state I was in? Two more surgeries followed over the course of the next several months because of complications, and Ken was never the same again. He had suffered enough brain trauma, along with the effects of the chemotherapy and radiation which followed, that his speech, his gait, and his cognitive skills were severely impacted. The musically gifted man with the beautiful singing voice could barely hold a note now.

When he was first diagnosed, we learned that only 14 percent of people in his age group (late 60s) live past eighteen months with a GBM. Dubbed the Terminator, GBM has no known cure but there were lots of different trials for brain tumors, including GBM, which offered hope for a cure. Distressingly, these doors were closed to Ken because all the traditional forms of treatment had not been exhausted. Even if they had been, he would have died waiting, his name having been placed at the bottom of a long list populated with the names of others just like Ken. The beast would not be stopped. Ken's immediate response had been to forego surgery or any form of treatment. He felt that this was his time; that God ordained it so and he was ready. However, I was not ready, and our kids were not ready, especially Ben. He needed time with his dad. So, reluctantly, Ken acquiesced to a grueling and horrifying ten months of procedures, surgeries, treatments, and hospital visits. Then his neuro-oncologist told him that it wasn't going to get better, so rather than continue to go through the torture of fighting a losing battle, Ken finally made the decision to stop and let nature take its course, and I had to agree that it was best. Ironically, I felt guilty for supporting Ken's wishes because there were family members who were less than supportive and even angry about it. It was the worst kind of Catch-22.

I found myself in the deepest, darkest valley of my life, trying desperately to keep my head above water with a fifty-pound weight tied to my waist, only to sink deeper and deeper into a dark and cold abyss. I'd always had Ken to lean on and weather storms with, but now I felt utterly alone. I didn't know what I was doing or where I was going. I depended on Ken for so many things in our marriage. He was the rock and steady force in our family, taking meticulous care of our finances, having been the financial director of NIH in the Washington area. Now he could no longer figure out how to use the remote control on the TV, let alone take care of our household finances. It was all up to me, and that filled me with terror. I fought this like crazy. I thought, *No, God! This is just too much! You can't be serious!* Up until the time he stopped treatment, which wasn't until six months after his diagnosis, I had to assume total responsibility, along with overseeing his complete care. Thank God for my son-in-law, Soon, who then took over the financial affairs, and for friends who jumped in to help here and there.

Ken couldn't sleep at night because of the massive amounts of steroids and he would get up at crazy hours and start cooking in the kitchen. He couldn't bathe by himself and when he tried, he would fall; and I, a petite, underweight five foot one-inch itty-bitty person, would have to pick up five foot ten inches of wet, dead weight, which was frightening for me. Then there was the incontinence and trying to get him to the bathroom in time, because he refused to wear disposable protection. On and on it went. I just couldn't believe the nightmare I was living. Things were so horrible that I didn't even have time to process the fact that the love of my life was going to die. I never stopped and thought about what life was going to be like a year hence, what I would do without him, how I would live, or would I even try to live. I cried myself to sleep every night and awoke each day to do it all over again just like the movie *Ground Hog Day*, but this wasn't funny.

IN THE EYE OF THE HURRICANE

When you find yourself in the middle of a hurricane, they say the eye of the storm is where you find your calm. I'm not sure that's a good metaphor for these kinds of storms in life. Unless, of course, the eye of the storm is where we find God and His peace. All I know is you're trapped in a situation where you have absolutely no control and no idea of when it's going to pass. A storm can come up so fast you don't even have time to mentally or physically prepare, as in the case of a tsunami or a tornado.

Despite the dire statistics I referred to earlier, in the beginning stages of Ken's mental deterioration, he underwent physical therapy, occupational therapy, and cognitive therapy in the hope that he could recover physically and mentally, should the tumor itself be controlled. Ken wanted very much to maintain some independence, so he would go out for walks in our neighborhood. We lived on a street that was a circle, and he was instructed by the warden (me) to stay on the circle and not deviate. One day, Ken had gone for a walk and I noticed that he'd been gone a lot longer than usual, so I went outside to find him. I looked frantically all over our neighborhood and he was nowhere to be found. There was a huge Catholic church just on the other side of our circle that he sometimes walked to and would stop to talk to the statue of Mary and give her a hug, until the priest came out one day to find out who he was and what was going on. Yes, he talked to the statue *and hugged it*! (Please note: Ken was not even Catholic!) When he told me about this little adventure, I told him please not to tell anyone he had a moment with the statue of Mary, or the people in white coats would be coming for him. We laughed. But this time he wasn't there.

A horrible fear swept over me and I was about to call the police, but the Lord put the thought in my head to drive out onto the main boulevard. I remembered that Ken once said he wanted to walk to Potomac Village which was a good three miles away, and he would have to take the boulevard to get there. Of course, I told him he couldn't because it was too far, but now I'm thinking *he doesn't remember things, his brain isn't working right.* I pulled out onto the busy street and headed toward the Village. I drove for a minute or so, and there he was, staggering and weaving into the street while drivers were honking and veering out of the way. They must have thought he was intoxicated. I pulled over and got him in the car, half scared out of my wits, and spent the rest of the day beating myself up for letting him go on walks by himself. That walk was the last one.

This was a lonely time. The only family I had locally were Ken, Rachel, and Ben who returned home when his dad had his first surgery. Watching his dad disintegrate right before his eyes, in his own fragile state, was more than he could handle, so he went to stay with close friends of ours who lived nearby. Thankfully, with our grandchildren in tow, the kids came over regularly to visit their Pop Pop, but they couldn't do what I had to do. It was just too overwhelming for them.

I desperately needed nighttime help so I could sleep and Ken would be safe in bed. However we were deeply in debt from ten years of criminal lawyers, rehabs, counselors, therapists, special schools, and a fancy prep-school bearing a price tag to match—our efforts from years of trying to help our son. Now we were unable to afford private care for Ken. My close friend Christy raised $50,000 in donations to cover our medical expenses and nursing care for Ken in the last two months of his life. During this time, friends brought meals or came to sit with him so I could go to the grocery store or just get a break. With this outpouring, I began to see that, even in the darkest, loneliest valleys, Jesus is there with His love and grace in ways that you'd never expect or experience otherwise.

Although I was living day to day in this dark and frightening valley with more pain than I could ever have imagined, a picture began to emerge. I began to see that there is a purpose for our valleys and, even more importantly, a purpose for the pain we experience there. At this point, it was just a tiny flicker, or snapshot, of something that I believe God wants us all to see when we go through catastrophic times and seasons. I was nowhere near where I needed to be to see the vastness of how God would redeem this nightmare.

GOD IS ON HIS THRONE

It was Mother's Day weekend and my brother, Gordon, and his wife, Jan, flew in from California and my sister Rhoda came down from New York to see Ken, knowing it would be their last time with him. We were all in the family room together talking when Rhoda looked at Ken and challenged, "Ken, where is God in all of this?" Neither of my siblings had a relationship with God, nor necessarily even believed that God exists. However, they know our family does believe and we've tried to live our faith out loud, in all our valleys, right before their eyes. Ken, as only he could do, looked Rhoda straight in the eye and without missing a beat declared, "He is on His throne!" My kids glanced at me and I just smiled thinking *that's my Mr. Wonderful* (how I often referred to him). Of course, he would say that he was simply stating the truth.

The story gets even better. Ken always used to say to Rachel, "Don't be average," and that stuck in her head for years. After all, her dad was far from average himself. He grew up in a poor family on the wrong side of the tracks, a black man in the segregated South, riding at the back of the bus (when he was lucky enough to have bus money), drinking from the designated water fountains, entering through back doors, picking tobacco and cotton to make some money for books, and going to bed with an empty belly on many nights. He made up his mind early that he was going to get out of the South and make something of himself. He knew that education was his ticket to social and economic freedom. The word *average* wasn't in Ken Stith's vocabulary, except to tell his daughter not to be that. Actually, he instilled that same attitude in all his kids—our two plus Saalik, his son from his first marriage.

Rachel was working for a direct sales company as a stylist selling and promoting their accessories. She'd worked her way up and now had a team of stylists under her. Every year, the company would sponsor a trip they awarded to their top stylists as an incentive to sell a certain amount in a given time-frame. This particular year, my Rachel was determined to earn that trip. The destination was Jamaica. Ken kept asking Rachel if she'd earned the trip yet, but she said she was only halfway to her goal of $45,000 worth of sales. Shortly after her father passed away, Rachel and I were talking about what he'd said to Rhoda, that God was on His throne. At that time, her company had just come out with engravable bar necklaces. The idea hit her: promote the necklace engraved with "On His Throne." Rachel posted her idea on social media, together with the story of Ken and Rhoda's exchange and a video chronicling the Stith family (previously made for us by a photographer friend). In almost no time, the "On His Throne" necklace was a huge hit. Even other stylists in the company were buying them. If I remember correctly, Rhoda herself bought one. Two days before the deadline, the gap was closing but she still needed $4,600 in sales to win her trip. Two nights later just before midnight, she did it. She ended up as the company's top seller that year, all because Ken said, "He's on His throne!" I wish he had lived long enough to know what happened.

THE FINGERPRINTS OF GOD

When you walk through the Valley of the Shadow of Death and look closely, you will see the fingerprints of God, the evidence that while you might feel alone, the truth is He's right there with you. These are the little signposts to remind us that God is in us and at work, even in our darkest times. In fact, those are the times when I think He shows up best, but I didn't see that so clearly then. The pain gets in the way of what's real and clouds our vision.

Within the span of just a few months, we celebrated our wedding anniversary, my birthday, Father's Day, and Ken's last birthday on the Fourth of July—each event, the last we would share together. Then, there was the worst week of all, leading up to the last week of Ken's life. Hospice had been helping by this time and I was scheduled for a five-day, desperately needed, respite after nine months of arduous caregiving. At that point, Ken was alert and eating. He had always been easy-going and pleasant, but now was overly fearful, resistant, and obsessive-compulsive about everything. He pleaded with me to let him stay at home. I tried to soothe and calm him. But I was sure this reprieve was the right thing for me to do, convinced I would be of no help to him if I had a mental breakdown. My daughter was furious with me, worried as she was about her dad and the care he'd receive. Looking back, I regretted my decision with every fiber of my being. The guilt I felt that week and later overwhelmed me. If I could relive that time and do it differently, I would; even though the end result may very well have been the same.

On the day before Ken was to return home from the nursing facility, he stopped eating and slept more and more. When he came home, he still wouldn't take food, only fluids. Then he wouldn't take fluids. The last thing he said to me was, "Hon, are you going to be okay?"

"Yes, Honey, I will," I lied. I held him in my arms, told him how much I loved him, and his eyes told me the same. Five days later he was in the presence of the Lord.

2

THE CLEAN UP

*Danger gathers upon our path. We cannot afford — we have no
right — to look back. We must look forward.*

—Winston Churchill

hat do you do when someone comes and drops a nuclear missile into the middle of your life? No warning. One day everything is as it should be and the next day all you see is chaos. That's what happens when someone goes through a devastating, life-altering experience. How do people who don't know the Lord manage? How do they survive the wreckage? At some point everyone experiences those valley times, but not everyone emerges from them better for it, more equipped and with more faith. In retrospect, I see that my relationship with Jesus has afforded me plenty of valley experiences— including excruciating pain from loss—which proved to be positive in the end. Of course, I didn't see that right away. It takes a while before you see the good in the evil. Does it seem shocking to even consider that there is ever any good to be found in evil that has been thrust upon you?

I didn't even see the missile coming. There was no newscast with dire predictions, so I had no time to prepare. It just hit, and that's exactly what it felt like from the day I took Ken to the ER in November of 2014 until I buried him. After that, I was left with all the debris to clean up.

Six hundred people filled the sanctuary at his memorial service, which was a testament to the man he was, much loved and appreciated by his family, his friends and his colleagues, all of whom came to honor his life. My friend Kathy, who was instrumental in Ken's coming to faith in Jesus so many years ago, came from the Midwest. The young kids he played basketball with all those years came. Longtime friends came from the West Coast, the North, and the South to pay their respects. Even his college frat brothers came, most of whom he hadn't seen since we were married back in 1980.

The burial was a military one with full honors, since Ken had spent twenty-six years of active duty in the Air Force before retiring as a colonel. My son Ben saved one of the spent shells from the twenty-one-gun salute fired at the burial site and had deflated his dad's basketball to place in the grave once Ken's body was lowered into the ground. I will never forget seeing the soldier start toward me, solemnly carrying the folded flag which had so grandly draped the coffin. In the few moments it took for him to walk the distance of a few hundred yards, it was as if a detached version of myself looked down upon the *me* who stood utterly broken in front of her husband's open grave. Then, he was there before me, handing me the flag. At that second, the out-of-body sensation left me and in its place, hot tears streamed down my face leaving traces of the sting of death. I screamed silently, *No!!! This isn't real! It's a mistake! He can't be gone!* Of course, no one heard my scream but God. Then my mother's stoicism kicked in. I forced my head up, determined to control my emotions and be the proud and dutiful wife saying goodbye to her beloved husband, with all the decorum I could muster. I had no idea what the hell I was doing, much less fathom what my life would be like when all the pomp and ceremony was over.

At the end of the reception and everyone went home, I was left with the mess: a life that was ripped from me, a dad taken from my kids, a grandfather my youngest grandchildren would never remember, and the loss of an identity I shared with Ken Stith for over thirty-five years. I was no longer married according to the guy in Death and Benefits at NIH where Ken had worked. As someone who had been a highly capable, "get it done" kind of girl, the one to whom everyone ran when they had a problem, these vulnerable feelings seemed strange, having not experienced them to this degree since I was a small child. Now I had no answers and I didn't even know what the questions were. There is a finality in death that renders us helpless.

LIFE IS MESSY

At home, my mantra was always, "A place for everything and everything in its place," a maxim originally coined by Benjamin Franklin and adopted as their motto by the Shakers. Ken used to say, that when I die, he would put that quote on my headstone, which we all thought would be so rolling-on-the-floor funny. Well, I guess he missed his opportunity. All that to say, I don't like when things are messy and out of place. But how could I possibly clean this one up? How do you escape the monster pain that takes over? You can't. How do you fix it? You can't. That's probably the first truth I learned on this journey. The consummate fixer can't fix this mess. This, and things like this, are bigger than we are and, no matter how we try, it just can't be fixed. There are no words to say, no formula to follow, and no way out except to put one foot in front of the other. Each day is a step forward toward healing. Some people might take medications or illicit drugs or turn to alcohol and stay stinking drunk. Others might eat themselves into oblivion with chocolate cake, but none of that will fix it. As soon as the buzz wears off or the chocolate cake is gone, the wall of pain confronts you head on. Our only recourse is God, leaning into the God of all comfort, since He's the only one who can heal our broken hearts. At the end of the day, God is way better than alcohol or drugs or chocolate cake, not to mention that there are no side effects or added pounds.

BEING ALONE

Surprisingly, even shockingly, nearly all my closest friends went MIA not long after the funeral was over. Silly me for assuming it would be otherwise, since I'd heard from others that it had happened to them. My telephone stopped ringing, the emails, texts, and condolences cards stopped coming. The silence was deafening. I always liked silence, but now, as if to punctuate the aloneness I felt, the only sounds were an occasional meow from my cats, Melody and Ashton, and the tick-tock of the clock in my office. My children had their own pain and grief to deal with, my mom had passed away two years prior, my dad was long gone, and I wasn't terribly close with either of my siblings who both lived far away. So, for the first time in my adult life I was completely and utterly alone. It's crazy and irrational, but I felt abandoned by everyone, even Ken. You see, feelings are not rational and rarely do they make sense.

As I reflect back on those early months, I think I needed to experience that lonely time, so that I would begin to depend on Jesus, instead of friends and family, to find myself. Yeah, I needed to find myself because, without Ken, I didn't know who I was. I didn't know Yolanda Cohen Stith. I didn't feel secure. This was the first time in sixty years that I wasn't *attached to* someone else for my sense of being. It would have been nice to have friends and family more present in my life during this time, but God had a higher purpose in their absence. It's natural that we look to others for comfort, support, and help; but for a Christian, our help comes from God and it's upon Him whom we need to rely. There are times in life when people are not available to us or maybe even no longer in our lives at all. Perhaps this is God's doing to lead us to a deeper dependency on Him. As I survey my past, there were many times that He took people out of my life for one reason or another and, ultimately, I knew that was why. That awareness didn't make it less hurtful, but it did help me to adjust my thinking about where and how my emotional needs get met. These are opportunities to progress from being a child to being an adult, and then back to being a child who has learned to rest in the Father's arms.

That pervading aloneness and solitude kept me in a fetal position for the first two years after Ken's death. Truthfully, had it not been for Rachel and Ben, I would have taken my own life. I thought about it a lot and I had plenty of opportunity, as I lay in bed night after night. Just thinking about pulling myself together, trying to make a new life as a sixty-year old single woman, and coping with the all-consuming grief was way too much. I was caught between two worlds —the world of my past with a husband who adored me and the world of an unknown future alone.

I attended a support group for spouses for three months, but I didn't find it very helpful, mostly because the group was not faith-based and everyone there was just drowning in their own agony with no way out. At least I had God. Then I went to see a grief therapist for a couple of months, but it was a waste of time, not to mention the twenty-dollar copay. She just sat there offering me tissue after tissue while I shared my story and vomited my pain all over her office each week. A year later, still in agony, I went through a program called Grief Recovery, which was more helpful but, in the end, I realized there was only one answer and one way to deal with this: to give myself permission to grieve for as long I needed to, in whatever way I needed to, depending on Jesus to be my anchor in the storm. I was going to have to let grief run the show, instead of me running the show. That was scary, because it meant not trying to control the untamable—the feelings of loneliness, despair, and fear. It meant not having a strategy for how to get the hell out of this valley and back on the mountaintop where the air is clear, and the view is grand. Of course, where there are mountaintops there are valleys.

RIDING THE GRIEF WAVE

Grieving is different for everybody. There are no rules. It's like riding the rapids on a raging river. You keep your safety vest (Jesus) securely fastened and hold on while you let the current take you where it will. Oh, and pray! You pray a lot. There are moments when the river is calm and quiet, which makes you wonder if you've reached the end of your grief; but then, all of a sudden, the current picks up, the rapids get crazy and there you go again, on that wild ride of emotions, up and down, trying to avoid the huge boulders and sharp-edged rocks along the way, not to mention the unpredictable drops at the falls. I've never been white water rafting, but I have a hell of an imagination! It's scary and you find yourself holding your breath as you approach those waterfalls, certain you will capsize and drown. Not that drowning would be such a bad thing in such an emotional state. And those rapids come out of nowhere, just like the emotional triggers that plummet you into the depths of your grief.

Countless nights would find me staring at the photograph of Ken at my bedside, tortured by the taunting reality that he's never coming back. This was not merely a bad dream from which I would wake up. This was excruciatingly real. He was never coming back. He's no longer in this world. It was final. I would sob until every ounce of energy in me was spent. Then I'd wake up the next morning and get hit in the face with the horrific reality all over again, like another nail pounded into my own coffin. There were movies I couldn't watch and music I couldn't listen to. Any remembrance of Ken sent me into the depths, and torrents of tears would flow. Yet I didn't want to forget him. I didn't want my life to move on without him, and I felt guilty in those rare moments when I felt any tiny bit of happiness or joy, as though I was betraying him. Crazy? Definitely, but that's all a part of the grieving process. It's not always rational and it doesn't always make sense. Again, your emotions are all over the place and the pain from your loss eclipses any modicum of rationality. All you know is you're hurting and there's nothing you can do to stop it, not even by eating a pint of mocha chocolate chip ice cream.

Grief is a multifaceted response to loss, particularly to the loss of someone with whom an intimate attachment was formed. Although society tends to focus primarily on the emotional response, grief also has physical, cognitive, behavioral, social, spiritual, and philosophical dimensions. While the terms are often used interchangeably, *bereavement* refers to the state of loss, and *grief* refers to the reaction to loss. *Grief* is a natural response. Jesus grieved. He grieved over His people and the unbelief in the city of Jerusalem (John 11:35 and Luke 19:41). While grief is commonly associated with death, we experience grief with other losses too, such as job loss, ill health, or the end of a relationship. Loss can be categorized as either physical or abstract, the physical loss being related to something that the individual can touch or measure, such as losing a spouse through death; while other types of loss are abstract and relate to aspects of a person's social interactions. Every step of the process is natural and healthy, having a beginning and an end. It is only when a person gets stuck in the grief journey for a long period of time that the grieving can become unhealthy, destructive, and detrimental.

In order to keep progressing through my own grief— and it took me a year or longer to even think about doing so —I had to be willing; willing to leave the past and build a future. My denial, my inability to accept that Ken was gone had kept me from moving forward. But now, I had to be willing to not be the wife of someone, the mother of someone, the daughter of someone, the friend of someone. I had to be willing to find my sense of stability and security *within* instead of seeking it in others. How do you do that? I had to leave that in God's hands and trust Him to do the building. *Well, Yolanda,* I reasoned to myself, *here you are in another valley, and while this valley may be deeper and darker than all the others combined, you are not alone here. It might feel that way, but the truth is God is with you because He is in you.* I knew that to be true. I knew from all the previous valleys in my life that when I seek the Lord there, I will experience the reality of His presence and love for me. His mercy and grace will lead me through it no matter how long I'm there, how bleak it is, or how hard it is for me to walk. No exceptions.

THE NEW SOCIAL NORM

In addition to grieving the loss itself, I had to deal with all the social ramifications of being unmarried; like not being invited to things because the event was for couples only. But one time, a friend invited me over for dinner along with two couples whom I didn't know. It was incredibly awkward for me as the fifth wheel or, in this case, the seventh wheel. After that, I decided I'd rather stay home than to go solo to a couple's party. Oh, and let's not forget all the "helpers" and their kind "encouragements," like, "Isn't it a blessing that you will see Ken again?" or "At least you had thirty-six years with him, more than some people get," or "You're still young. You will find someone and remarry." These idiotic platitudes and bumper sticker slogans were anything but helpful. Death and grief are really hard for others to deal with and they often just don't know what to say, so they say dumb things. Truthfully, I'm sure I've done it myself, although I don't remember ever saying any of those things to a woman who just buried her husband. Then there were those who tried to bring me comfort by telling me how devastated they were when their eight-five-year-old grandmother died or their fifteen-year-old Labrador retriever died. I understand that death is painful, regardless of who you lose, but comparing the death of your eighty-five-year-old grandparent or your dog to the early death of one's spouse? Sorry, it's not the same.

By the end of year two, I began to experience a shift. It came so slowly and so gradually that it took several months to even notice it. I began to enter into a phase of acceptance and began to find the good in my circumstances. I don't mean that it was good that my husband died, but I sensed the goodness of God in my pain and loss. Deep down, I'd known it was there. I just needed to wipe away my tears, open my eyes, and begin to seek it. "Blessed are those who mourn for they will see God" (Matthew 5:4). So true. As the shift in my outlook started to emerge, I began to trust the Lord to provide what I needed each day, whether it was encouragement, companionship, or financial help, and He did. I was surprised by the friends whom I hadn't expected to step in, but who suddenly appeared in my life as an extension of God's heart and hands. The friendships that were there all along grew deeper and became more mean-ingful to me. Yes, the Lord was there, and He was taking care of me in countless ways and I began discovering, in a much greater way than I ever could have before, that my identity was so much more than being Mrs. Kenneth W. Stith or checking "married" on a government form.

If you've ever had to bury your spouse, you know exactly what I'm talking about. It's like losing a leg and learning how to get around without it. The problem is that we live in a world that isn't equipped to accommodate singlehood any more than it is equipped to accommodate amputees. When you go to church and see all the families—

Dad and Mom and the kids—and all the programs for the families, you begin to feel disconnected, like being unmarried is a disease or a handicap. This was new territory for me, and I really didn't know what to do with it. It was just another challenge to try to overcome, another problem to solve. Some stop going to church and other venues where there are constant reminders that they don't fit in. Instinctively, I knew that was not the answer for me, although I didn't know what was.

I've had friends who have had similar circumstances, but after a short time of being alone, they hopped on a dating site, and met and married their new prince charming, so they wouldn't have to be alone anymore. I completely get it, because grieving the loss of your spouse and the life you once had, as well as learning to be single again . . . well, it doesn't get any lonelier than that. But, for me, there is no replacement for Ken. I won the lottery when he came into my life. The funny thing about God, though, is that He isn't fond of our making decisions apart from Him, about what we will and will not allow. After forty years of walking with God, I should know better than to say never. So, He began dealing with my unwillingness to allow Him to direct and build my future.

I thank God every day for the blessing Ken was to me for thirty-six years. I realized that Ken was a gift from God to me and to my kids and grandkids. I can't limit God and what He might have for me in the future, so I am moving forward with open hands and heart to see what He might put there. It's just possible that I might have to make room in my life for the unexpected. So, I continue to clean up the mess that was left of my heart and soul by trusting God to heal me.

3

THE BROKEN ROAD

*In the shadow of death may we not look back to the past, but seek
in utter darkness the dawn of God.*

—Pierre Teilhard de Chardin, S.J.

I had a life before God and before Ken danced his
way in, or at least I thought I did. It was more
like a broken road, a road paved with discontentment, the
landscape marked by bad choices. What I didn't know was
that *real* life comes from God. Although, too many are
completely unaware that something is even missing from
their lives, others spend their lives searching for that
missing piece in a person who will make them happy or in
that ultimate illumination that will fulfill them. As for me, I
knew there was something missing and I was in search of it,
even though I didn't know what it was or where to look.

My life changed pretty dramatically when Jesus pulled

me out of the gutter and off the broken road. For some, the change isn't outwardly dramatic because their pre-Jesus days might not have *looked* rebellious, though apart from Christ, we are all rebels. They might have grown up in church, praying around the dinner table, attending Bible studies, and going on youth mission trips. That was not my pre-Jesus experience, not even close. In fact, I was so rebellious and hedonistic that when I found God, my older brother (no saint himself), said at one point that I'd gone from being the black sheep in the family to being the golden child. According to my brother, who swears he's not an atheist, my spiritual transformation was quite a one-eighty.

My parents, Mickey and Irene Cohen, were first generation Jewish Americans; both their parents having fled Russia in their youth to escape rampant persecution, and settling in Baltimore, Maryland where both my parents grew up. Much later—sometime in the forties—a scandal broke out involving my paternal grandfather and all the Cohens escaped to LA before I was even born. By the time I was born in LA, Rhoda was already six years old and Gordon was two. That made me the baby.

I grew up in a Conservative Jewish home where the practice of Jewish customs was a high priority for my mother Irene, whom we often called Sergeant Cohen. My dad had no interest. It was Irene who made sure I went to synagogue every week for the Sabbath (called Shabbat), plus Sunday school and Hebrew school. When I was eleven, I met with the rabbi in preparation for my becoming a Bat Mitzvah (Daughter of the Law). This too was at the bidding of Irene, of course. It was, after all, her way or the highway. Later, I took the highway, but I'll get to that.

My paternal grandmother, whom I saw almost every weekend, was my main source of acceptance growing up.

Her house was my place of refuge where I loved to go and spend the night. Although I like to think I was her favorite, I shared that distinction with my brother Gordon. Apart from Gram, it wasn't a terribly happy childhood for any of us, and each of us dealt with our wounds in different ways. Rhoda moved out of the house, got a job and eventually, moved to New York City where she has remained her entire life. Gordon graduated from high school, joined the Army in the late sixties, and was discharged for going AWOL. He adopted the counter-culture ideology of the day, both socially and politically, embracing Marxism as his religion of choice, though he might take exception to that last point.

My elementary school experiences weren't exactly happy ones either. I would routinely get in trouble for talking too much and, back then, disciplinary actions included shaming. I was made to sit in the corner and was even paddled by the principal once. But there was at least one happy memory: my fifth-grade teacher, Miss Wilson, was the first to recognize that I had artistic talent. In fact, I credit her for starting me on a path to developing my artistry and using it to inspire others throughout my adult life. Mrs. Wilson once asked me to paint a picture for her boyfriend. As it happened, her boyfriend just happened to be the TV actor Bill Bixby!

Later, I ended up following my big brother's footsteps into the world of drugs and a hippie lifestyle. I wanted nothing whatsoever to do with religion, much less the one crammed down my throat by Irene. Here is where I took the highway and headed to Boulder, Colorado. It was in Boulder that I rushed into a marriage with my high school boyfriend that never should have happened. The marriage didn't last. Alone and depressed, I tried to take my own life by turning on the gas oven in my apartment. This Valley

Girl was a mess. No goals and no desire to live. I was estranged from my parents at this point and without any friends in Colorado. The ex got the friends (okay, they were his friends to begin with) and most of my amazing record collection.

My personal life may have been in shambles, but the retail chain I worked for promoted me to manage one of their stores which meant a move to Rapid City, South Dakota. It was February of 1979. Some promotion, huh? It was the dead of winter and everywhere I looked was white and stayed that way well into late spring. I didn't realize it then, but I was on a collision course with God.

I looked for meaning in relationships, sex, drugs, my job, and having fun. Only it wasn't fun. I found myself pregnant and did what lots of women do. I aborted the inconvenience and tried to tell myself that it was for the best, but deep down inside I knew I murdered my child and it was wrong. I could have had the baby and given him up for adoption to a couple who were unable to conceive, but that would have been too great a sacrifice on my part, and far too noble. It was much easier to just quietly get rid of the problem. It took me years to forgive myself for that.

It was during that time that my roommate invited me to go with her to church on Easter Sunday. Her sister in-law, a born-again Christian, had invited her and she didn't want to go without reinforcements. I guess, being a Catholic, she felt she was safe with a Jew. I had never been inside a church and, frankly, I was a little curious.

Debbie and I sat toward the back of the little Lutheran church and after his sermon, the Pastor invited the congregation to come to the front, row by row, to take communion. Communion? What the heck is that? Debbie didn't want to go down front because she was Catholic. Non-practicing, but her Catholic guilt was as strong a motivator as my Jewish guilt! Regardless, I felt compelled—even drawn —to go to the front. I was the last person on the row to be served. Kneeling down at the altar, I found myself praying and asking God to forgive me for, basically, my entire life, including aborting my child. I heard Jesus say to me that He was my Messiah and because of Him I'm forgiven. That's when I broke down. By the time Pastor Dahlstrom came to me with the bread and wine, I was sobbing my eyes out. He seemed a bit unsure of what to do with me, this being a mainline denominational church, unaccustomed to emotional displays in their services.

THE DISCO

Living in Rapid City, South Dakota, was anything but culturally stimulating and fun. Yes, there is Crazy Horse and Mount Rushmore, but the Black Hills were all a bit anti-climactic after living in the foothills of the Colorado Rockies. But what happens next creates a crazy juxtaposition of place and divine destiny that changes everything.

It was the late 1970s and disco was all the rage, no less so in Rapid City. Everyone went to the Galaxy Disco Club on Friday and Saturday nights. I was there with my roommate on this particular night, dancing and having a good time, when I was asked to dance by a definitely-not-my-type guy in a white polyester suit and big platform shoes. If you have a picture in your mind of John Travolta in Saturday Night Fever, then you're on the right track, except, oh, he was the Afro-American version. I soon learned his name was Ken Stith and he was a captain in the Air Force, stationed at nearby Ellsworth AFB. We danced a couple of times and he asked for my phone number. I was young and dumb, so I gave it to him. Little did I know at the time, but that night, when he spotted me on the dance floor, he told his buddy he was going to marry me.

THE BLACK MESSIAH IN PLATFORMS

Sure enough, he called and asked me out. We ended up at the Ponderosa Steak House for our first date. I admit I was a little disappointed. I expected something a little more upscale from this guy. But still, the following day, flowers came to the store I managed, and they came every day that week. Who wouldn't fall for a guy like that?

In the same year that I met Messiah Jesus, I fell for Ken, not that the two should be confused. We had absolutely nothing in common. He was a Republican and I was a Democrat. He was a conservative and I was a liberal. He was an officer in the military and I was a hippie. He grew up in abject poverty and went to university and graduate school and I was the manager of a women's retail store and graduated from the school of hard knocks with a little bit of college here and there, mostly there. He didn't even have a toilet in his little, post-war house, and I grew up in LA with a heated swimming pool in my backyard. Granted, it was a modest little bungalow and we didn't live in Beverly Hills and most everyone in Southern California had a pool. I was a Valley Girl. He loved Motown. I loved late sixties and seventies classic rock which epitomized the era. We were as different as two people could possibly be!

My parents stopped speaking to me when I wrote and told them I was dating a black man and it was getting serious. It was bad enough that he wasn't Jewish, but being black is not something you can change, unless you're Michael Jackson. This is the mind-set born out of a racially divided city like Baltimore where they both grew up. If I were forced to choose between Ken and them, I would choose Ken. I knew in my heart that God brought this *mensch* (Yiddish for *fine person*) into my life.

We got married and had our first child within a year's time. It wasn't until Rachel was almost two years old that my parents began speaking to me. My mom decided to come and visit me in Omaha, Nebraska, where Ken was now stationed. She wasn't ready to meet Ken yet and I respected that. She and I needed some time of forgiveness and reconciliation anyway, and this visit proved to be a cathartic one for both of us and a turning point in our relationship. It wasn't long after that, maybe a year later, that both my mom and my dad were ready to meet Ken while we were out in LA on business. All their petty racial prejudices and imagined stereotypes flew out the window when they got to know him and realized he was a man of impeccable character. He also had more education than anyone in the entire Cohen Family, It didn't take long before Ken became their favorite, and in their eyes he walked on water. I was just chopped liver.

MY NEW LIFE

Some people's path to salvation is motivated by their fear of going to hell and that's not a bad reason, since the Scriptures describes it as a place of eternal separation from God. But my search had less to do with that, and more to do with a peace that eluded me all of my life, a peace that meant I no longer had to be afraid. There was nothing but inner turmoil in my childhood and my early adult years. So when I came to the Lord, and began to grow in knowledge and understanding, I began to experience a peace that I had never known.

Nobody seemed to understand what happened to me on that Easter Sunday in the late seventies in the little Lutheran Church in Rapid City, not even I; at least not until I met my new friend Kathy after Ken and I moved to Omaha. Upon meeting her, I quickly learned that I'd had a rebirth experience.

"Stay away from Kathy Caruso!" said the woman at my new workplace. "She's one of those born-again Christians!" Of course, I made a beeline for Kathy's office and introduced myself. I blurted out breathlessly that I was Jewish but believed in Jesus and that I needed some help figuring it all out. Unfortunately, most people think being Jewish is based on religion, as opposed to one's birthright through the Patriarchs: Abraham, Isaac, and Jacob. Jewish people believe that you can be a Buddhist and remain Jewish, but you cannot be a Jesus follower and remain Jewish, which makes no sense.

Kathy and I became fast friends. I was her new project. She bought me a Bible and a book about other Jewish people who also believed Jesus was the Messiah. Until then, I thought I was the only Jew who believed in Jesus. Imagine my surprise to discover that there were thousands at that time. Through my relationship with Kathy, I began to grow spiritually as a Jewish believer.

MY FIRST ENCOUNTER WITH CHRIST

I'd grown up in a mixed Jewish and Gentile neighborhood and even though the Sergeant didn't like me playing with the Gentile kids, I did anyway. The first time I heard the term *kike* was when two of the Gentile boys in my neighborhood called me a Christ-killer kike and dropped a giant snail down the back of my shirt and smashed it. I ran home crying and asked my mom who Christ was and what a *kike* was. All she said was to stay away from those *goyim* (Gentiles). I was taught to distrust Gentiles who were, in the Jewish mind, synonymous with Christians. If you weren't Jewish or Muslim, then you were Christian. For most first-generation Jewish-Americans, it was them and us. So, years later, I was devastated when one of our friends at church accusatorily told me that "my people" (the Jews) killed Jesus. I knew that Jesus gave up His life willingly for the purpose of saving *all* mankind—both Jews and Gentiles. Since I was studying both the Old and New Testaments and church history, I knew their attitude was a reflection of centuries of Roman Catholic hatred of the people of the Bible. Sadly, even today within the Church, many of those same attitudes remain. Perhaps not quite as overtly, but it can be seen in subtle ways.

Church was a very foreign place for Jewish believers. For the most part, Glad Tidings Assembly of God was a warm and inviting place. My friend's ignorant comment notwithstanding, this church had a heart for Israel and prayed regularly for the Jewish people. The first time Ken and I attended Glad Tidings we were guests of Kathy and her husband Joe. It wasn't their home church, but there was a special service this particular Friday night featuring a retired Air Force officer as the guest speaker who came to share about his time serving in the Israeli Defense Force, flying helicopters as a volunteer. Why, you might ask, would he volunteer to put his life in harm's way for a country that was not his own? In fact, this man was not even Jewish, but he had a heart for Israel and the Jewish people—God's chosen people—and considered this his ministry to them. I knew I was home when we walked into the church and the entire congregation was singing *Shalom Aleichem* (translated *peace be unto you*), a traditional Hebrew song sung on Shabbat in every synagogue around the world. Mind you, this was a congregation filled with non-Jewish believers, all clapping and singing. Of course, as an Air Force officer himself, Ken paid rapt attention. It was in that church the following Sunday morning that God not only had Ken's attention, but He had his heart as well. He went down to the altar at the conclusion of the service seeking prayer with one of the church leaders. He was a great guy before that day, but after he gave his life to Jesus, he became a driven, passionate, and committed follower of the Jewish Messiah.

THE LEVI CONNECTION

One of God's gifts to me and my family was Walt Levi. Walt was an elderly Jewish man who immigrated to the United States after fleeing Nazi Germany in the late thirties—no easy feat. He had a twin sister who went to Israel, but Walt and his brother came here with their wives. Walt ultimately lost his entire family of origin in the Holocaust, with the exception of his two siblings. But in spite of the tyranny of hatred and evil against the six million Jews whose lives were exterminated, and its horrific impact on the Levi family, Walt found his Messiah and the forgiveness and healing that goes with that. He and his wife ended up at Glad Tidings where they were loved and cared for by the congregation. Walt became an adopted member of our family. I was still estranged from my parents at the time, and he was like a father to both Ken and me, and a grandfather to my daughter Rachel. He had Shabbat dinner with us every Friday night and was a member of the small Messianic Jewish fellowship that met in our home. Before we moved from Omaha to our next duty station, Walter gave us, as a parting gift, his now-late wife's solid brass candlestick holders and his sterling silver wine goblet After all these years, I still use them for holidays or a Shabbat meal.

DEVOURING THE BIBLE

When I started reading the Old and New Testaments, I was floored to discover all the prophecies concerning the Messiah: His lineage, details about His birth, His life and His death. I was especially floored by God's references to Himself as a compound unity, or God in three persons. I wondered, haven't the rabbis seen these passages of Scripture? If someone like me—uneducated in biblical Hebrew, Aramaic, and Greek—could read the Scriptures and see so clearly, why on earth couldn't those who were trained to study the Scriptures see what was so obvious? That's the million-dollar question that has only two possible answers —spiritual blindness and a hard heart.

Thus says the Lord, 'Let not a wise man boast of his wisdom, and let not the mighty man boast of his might, let not a rich man boast of his riches; but let him who boasts boast of this, that he understands and knows Me, that I am the Lord who exercises lovingkindness, justice and right-eousness on earth; for I delight in these things,' declares the Lord. (Jeremiah 9:23-24)

Reading the Bible to know God and to understand the wisdom in His Scriptures became a passion for me, an odyssey of study and spiritual awakening both as a child of God and a Messianic Jew. The Scriptures and my newfound faith gave meaning and depth to my heritage, my physical birth, and my spiritual life as a Jew; all of which meant very little to me prior to knowing the Jewish Messiah. In a retrospective frame of mind, I told my mom, years after I became I believer, how thankful I was that she insisted that I become a Bat Mitzvah. Oh, and I almost forgot! Five years later, in suburban Washington, when we were attending a Messianic Jewish Congregation, I ended up leading a B'nai Mitzvah class, teaching the kids how to read and write Hebrew. Their Bar and Bat Mitzvahs meant a lot to my own two kids. I didn't have to make them do it; they chose to because they saw it as a meaningful part of their spiritual formation. Well, maybe they wanted a party, too.

Many years after my spiritual awakening and the reconciliation with my parents, I would often have conversations with my mom about spiritual matters like life after death and things in the Old Testament that I knew she didn't know. She loved Jewish history and began working as a docent at the Skirball Cultural Center in Los Angeles, a prestigious museum of all things Judaica. Her time there piqued her interest in the Old Testament, which for Jewish people is the only Bible they recognize. Of course, they do not refer to it as the Old Testament.

One day, my mom and I were having a conversation about death, my favorite subject (since it's a great segue to talking about life) and she claimed there was no such thing as life after death. I asked her how she knew that and, of course, she had no concrete foundation for her reasoning; so I challenged her to read the Jewish Scriptures. To my mind, placing all your confidence in your own opinion, when eternity hangs in the balance, is just plain dumb! I sent her a Bible, plus she had one of her own she bought at Skirball, and she began reading, starting in the first chapter of Genesis. I sent her all the Scripture references about the Messiah and told her to make a note of those, when she got to them. Whenever we were together over the next nine years, we would read and then discuss what she had read. We talked about the Fall of Man, the Levitical priesthood and its sacrificial system, the Patriarchs, Israel's kings, then straight into the Prophets. I let my mom interpret what she was reading, which she did very well. My personal belief is that the Scriptures are not hard to understand, unless you come to them with a bias and try to make them fit into your own world view. When we came to the last three verses of chapter 52 through the end of chapter 53, about the Suffering Servant, I mentioned to her that this is the only chapter that is *never* read in the synagogue. She found that very interesting. So had I when I discovered that truth. The entire book of Isaiah is read in the synagogue, except for this one chapter. Hmmm, what's that about? My mother wondered the same thing. I asked her who the Suffering Servant was. She put down her Bible and looked me straight in the eye, her quest to understand, or possibly refute, what I'd been telling her for years, now over; and said "Okay, it's true. Yeshua is the Messiah. I see that now." She did not come to this conclusion impulsively. She came to that conclusion on the heels of nine years of systematic study from the Book of Genesis straight through the Prophets. I would even go as far as saying that she didn't want it to be true. She didn't want Jesus to be the Jewish Messiah, but when God opened her eyes, she couldn't deny it. I asked her if she wanted to pray and ask Him to give her life. She did.

My mom was far from stupid. She didn't need a college education to plainly see what was in her own Bible. The problem with most Jewish people is that we are taught that

Jesus is not for *us*, He is for *them*, the Gentiles, and to believe in Him is to convert to another religion and no longer be Jewish. Nothing could be further from the truth. That is nothing but Jewish propaganda—an emotional reaction stemming from the Church's anti-Semitism and persecution of the Jewish people for the past two thousand years. There is nothing that makes more sense than for a Jewish person to embrace the Jewish Messiah and enter into a covenant that was made with *them*, and which includes anyone who would believe in Israel's Messiah! This new covenant is not the beginning of a religion; it's the restitution of a relationship between God and man. Truthfully, most Gentiles don't get it either.

My mom was in her late seventies when she went from spiritual death to life and, although she didn't really walk it out for very long, I did see a softening in the last twenty years of her life. My dad had not been happy about all the Bible studying going on, afraid that my mom would convert. The spiritual interference in that household was apparent—a real battle for their minds. However, when my mom gave her life to Yeshua (Jesus), she urged my dad to listen to what I had to say, and he did (he was afraid not to). About a year later, after some of his friends died and he himself suffered a mild stroke, we prayed together, and he too became a believer.

At the end of my mother's life, following years of advanced dementia, I prayed with her to let go and go home to the Lord. Four hours later she was gone, but I know where she is today, and I look forward to seeing her again. My mom and dad gave me physical life, and I had the great blessing and joy of leading them to eternal life!

It was the Broken Road that led me to the best-kept secret in the Jewish world—Messiah Jesus. Had everything been great in my life up until then, had I come from a loving, nurturing, and functional family, and found contentment in the superficial things in life; would I have found my way to the Lord? Only God knows, but I think it was the broken pieces of my life—the detours, the failures, and the potholes along the way—that revealed my need for God. If we don't recognize our need, then we will continue to live with the gods of our own making—self or someone, or something else. Coming to know Jesus personally, in a way that leads you to a new life, is the greatest gift that God can give you. But once we become His children through our rebirth experience, coming to know Him as our life is even greater and *this* is a lifelong experience. He's not just our Savior and Lord, He is our very Life—Yeshua H'u Chaiyim!

4

THE DECEIVER

*There are two equal and opposite errors into which our race can
fall about the devils. One is to disbelieve in their existence.
The other is to believe, and to feel an excessive
and unhealthy interest in them.*

—C. S. Lewis

*J*esus referred to the devil as the Deceiver,
because that is his character and the primary
way he operates. Once we become children of
God by receiving His life through Jesus Christ (see John
1:12-13), we become a threat to Satan and his plan to usurp
God's authority, power, and praise. The best way for him to
do that is to keep us from glorifying God by controlling
what we believe, since beliefs lead to choices and how we
live our lives. "Or do you not know that your body is a
temple of the Holy Spirit who is in you, whom you have

from God, and that you are not your own? For you have been bought with a price; *therefore, glorify God in your body*" (1 Corinthians 6:19-20, emphasis added). Now we become a target; whereas, prior to our spiritual conversion, evil already had control over us and there was nothing about us that was remotely threatening.

Satan and his host of demons are enemies of God, and now our enemies; however, Satan was defeated at the cross when Jesus died and rose from the grave.

[God] raised [Jesus] from the dead, and seated Him at His right hand in the heavenly places, *far above all rule and authority and power and dominion, and every name that is named*, not only in this age, but also in the one to come. And *He put all things in subjection under His feet, and gave Him as head over all things to the church*, which is His body, the fullness of Him who fills all in all. (Ephesians 1:20-22, emphasis added)

As a result of Christ's death, burial, and resurrection, the power of the Evil One has been rendered powerless in the lives of Christians unless, of course, they are deceived into giving him access and control. In Christ, we have been given power and authority over evil and the Adversary knows this, but do we?

THE DUMB THINGS VALLEY GIRLS DO

Prior to my encounter with Jesus on the broken road, I had been involved in some occult activity. Initially, I preface this story with an incident that happened not long before that. One night I was with some friends; getting high and doing stupid things up in the Hills where the famous Hollywood sign is. It had been raining all week, a rarity for LA, so the ground was wet. Someone dared the driver of an off-road vehicle to drive perpendicularly up the mountain to the top with three of us in his car who were just as stupid as he was. I sat in the front seat, buckled in, and up we went. Did it ever occur to me that this wasn't going to work, and if it didn't work, what might happen? Okay, that day I was a *really* dumb Valley Girl! The Jeep was just about at the top when the wheels started to spin. The more the driver tried to get control, the worse it got. Now the Jeep was sideways and slipping and the driver screamed for everyone to get out. They did, except for me. I was buckled into my seat and didn't have enough time to get out, so down I went hundreds of feet, rolling down the mountainside. The canvas top flew off and with every roll, my head hit the rocks all the way down the canyon, until it stopped. Fortunately, there was a roll bar on the car, which is why I'm here telling the story.

I was in and out of consciousness on the way down, but I remember thinking that I was going to die. I was eighteen years old. My first thought was about God and then my family, my life, and that it was going to be over any second. The reason I'm sharing this story is because I *knew* that it was God who spared my life. I didn't know why, and I certainly didn't know who He was, but this knowledge became the catalyst for me to find Him.

FACE-TO-FACE WITH EVIL

A close friend told me about her mom and a metaphysical group that she attended once a week in the Valley that I might be interested in checking out. She knew that I was on a spiritual quest and thought this might be helpful. I talked with her mom and got the leader's contact information and called her. She was a self-described religious practitioner, a seemingly lovely woman with a welcoming persona. She invited me to come to her home and join the group. Her name was Carmel Nicks who happened to be the aunt of Stevie Nicks. This was just prior to Stevie joining Fleetwood Mac.

There were about eight other women present at the first meeting I attended. They were much older than my nineteen years. Carmel gave me a book about metaphysics and reincarnation to read. I looked to her as a mentor. Little did I know that I was headed for dangerous waters, but God knew, and, in retrospect, I know He had His hand of protection upon me. They opened up their meeting in prayer by calling on so-called spirit guides and inviting them to lead. Next, one of the women performed something I had never heard of or seen before. She had a tablet of lined paper and a pen. She closed her eyes, prayed to her spirit guide (I can't remember who it was—Ulysses S. Grant or John the Baptist), and with her eyes tightly closed, she began asking questions and her hand began to write the answers on the lines in perfect penmanship covering a full page! It was a totally different style of handwriting from her own. My eyes grew as big as saucers, the hair on the back of my neck stood up, and I knew that something very weird was going on in this house and with this group. Still I was intrigued, so I continued to show up.

One day, Carmel asked me to stay after one of the meetings because she wanted to pray with me about a spirit guide of my own. As we sat alone together, she asked, "What about Jesus as your spirit guide?" I said that wouldn't work for me because Jews don't believe in Jesus. Then she suggested Moses and I didn't have any issues with him. With eyes closed, Carmel prayed and invited Moses to come and be my spirit guide. I can't remember now if she asked Mo to come in me or just guide me, but nothing happened. No Mo, no nothing. I couldn't get a spirit guide. Bummer, or so I thought at the time. Carmel said not to worry, that maybe it will just take a little time and more prayer. Am I questioning any of this yet? No. I didn't have anything good or bad to say about it at this point. Oy, a Valley Girl, indeed!

Carmel and her husband were going out of town one weekend and she asked me if I would stay at her house and take care of her two dogs. I told her I'd be happy to, so I came over on Friday with a weekend bag of clothes, watched some TV, and got ready for bed after taking the dogs out one last time for the night. I hopped into bed and shut off the light. All of a sudden, I felt like someone was in the room with me, watching me. I sat up and looked into the darkness and felt "a presence" move across the room. I could sense that it was evil. I turned on the light but still felt like there was something wrong, something cold and dark, and I was filled with terror. I threw on my clothes, grabbed my bag, and high-tailed it out of Carmel's house. I only went back twice a day to walk her dogs to fulfill my obligation and I never went back again. The only positive thing that came from my relationship with Carmel was coming to the realization that evil exists, that it has a source and is nothing to joke about. Oh, and an invitation backstage at a Fleetwood Mac concert when they were at their best!

I realized that Carmel and her group were involved in something that was the very antithesis of God. Many years later, when my eyes and my heart were opened to Jesus, I knew that it had been the occult and that God protected me from any demonic spirit (in the person of Mo or otherwise) who would gain control over me. God had His own plans for my life.

As a child, I was always afraid of the dark, but the events at the Nicks' house only exacerbated it. Even after I became a believer, met and married Ken, and began to grow spiritually, my fear of the dark continued to grow. I kept lights on at home and I didn't like staying alone at night when Ken was traveling. This fear became so great that when Ken had to go away to Air War College for three months, I begged him to let me go with him rather than stay at home by myself. A door in my life had been opened and the Evil One had set up what the Bible calls a *stronghold*. The word *stronghold* is found once in the New Testament, used metaphorically by Paul in a description of the Christian's spiritual battle:

For though we live in the world, we do not wage war as the world does. The weapons we fight with are not the weapons of the world. On the contrary, they have divine power to demolish *strongholds*. (2 Corinthians 10:3-4, emphasis added)

What are these strongholds we face? In the very next verse, Paul interprets the metaphor: "We demolish arguments and every pretension that sets itself up against the knowledge of God, and we take captive every thought to make it obedient to Christ" (2 Corinthians 10:5). The "arguments" are the philosophies, reasonings, and schemes of the world. The "pretensions" have to do with pride, man-centeredness, and self-sufficiency. Strongholds can manifest in all sorts of ways—sexual addictions and abuse, drug and alcohol addiction, family trauma, and pride, to name a few. The Enemy is firmly entrenched in these strongholds, with erroneous beliefs and lies, which keep us from living out of God's truth. They must be broken.

At this time, I didn't know that I had authority and power in Jesus over the Enemy or that he had to flee at my command. Who knew? Once I saw what the Scriptures said about these things, the game was over. I renounced my past involvement with the occult and told the demons that they were trespassing on God's property! I haven't experienced fear and terror of darkness or evil since. Jesus broke that stronghold when I prayed, and the demons knew that *I knew* my position in Jesus now. In his letter to the Colossians Paul says:

For in Him all the fullness of Deity dwells in bodily form, and in Him you have been made complete, and He is the head over all rule and authority; and in Him you were also circumcised with a circumcision made without hands, in the removal of the body of the flesh by the circumcision of Christ; having been buried with Him in baptism, in which you were also raised up with Him through faith in the working of God who raised Him from the dead. And when you were dead in your transgressions and the uncircumcision of your flesh, He made you alive together with Him, having forgiven us all our transgressions, having canceled out the certificate of debt consisting of decrees against us and which was hostile to us; and He has taken it out of the way, having nailed it to the cross. *When He had disarmed the rulers and authorities, He made a public display of them, having triumphed over them through Him.* (Colossians 2:9-15, emphasis added)

In 1 John 5:18 we are told that the Adversary cannot make us do anything or control us in any way. He does, however, try to get us to believe things that aren't true, just as he did with the first man and woman in the Garden of Eden. Here's how he does it:

- Presents some truth mixed with lies

- Uses our feelings to validate erroneous thoughts and lies
- Distorts, manipulates, and tempts

First, not every thought that comes to your mind is *your* thought; meaning it may or may not have been generated by you. The Evil One will present your mind with thoughts, seemingly benign, but craftily calculated with evil intent to lead you away from the truth, God's truth. Let me define God's truth: Anything that God says about you, Himself, others, and life in general. The bottom-line is what God says is true whether your feelings agree or not, whether it makes sense or not, and whether it conflicts with what you've learned in the past or not.

Second, your feelings will not tell you what's true; they only tell you what you *believe* to be true, so you can't rely on them. Feelings have a purpose, but it's not to tell you what to believe or what you should do; they simply react to your experiences both positive and negative. If you had positive experiences with cats growing up, when you see a cat now, you will feel something positive about it; and conversely, if you've had negative experiences with cats, you might feel something negative upon seeing it.

Lastly, the Deceiver will distort events and things people say and do; and manipulate you by getting you to rely on your feelings to purposely trigger a lie. That lie is something you've believed from the time you were a child; a lie that he helped you believe in the first place. All this is done so you will react by "walking after the flesh," that is, your version of the flesh—how you protect yourself and get your emotional or spiritual needs met apart from God. Romans 8:6-8 says, "For the mind set on the flesh is death, but the mind set on the Spirit is life and peace, because the mind set on the flesh is hostile toward God; for it does not subject itself to the law of God, for it is not even able to do so, and those who are in the flesh cannot please God."

Our defense against the schemes of the Evil One is God's truth. Jesus said in John 8:32, "You shall know the truth, and the truth shall make you free." We get to choose what we are going to believe. We get to choose how we are going to respond to the Adversary and the lies he triggers. When we don't choose the truth and instead believe the lies, we will, most certainly, choose our own fleshly resources to protect ourselves and live independently of Christ. It is in this way that we create even more suffering for ourselves.

THE EVIL ONE'S MO

I remember the first time I recognized a thought that came to my mind and knew it was not generated by me. It was not the most heinous or evil thought, but it had an evil intention. My husband was paying the bills one evening at the kitchen table, rather than at his office where he later started doing it. Ken's career path had led him into finance by this time and he was a stickler for making sure every-thing was accounted for in our accounts, right down to the last penny. Typically, at least back at this particular time, he would get in a really foul mood while paying the bills and reconciling the bank statements. I always stayed clear of him at those times because I knew by his tone and body language, and the pervading quiet taking over, that he wasn't happy. I was walking within earshot to head upstairs to my office when he stopped me to ask yet another a question about a specific charge on one of our credit cards. "What's this charge?" he challenged. I didn't like his tone, nor did I like what felt like interrogation, as if I was out spending money recklessly on fifteen pairs of shoes. He should know better than that. Just after he questioned me and I responded, the thought, *"You jerk,"* came into my mind. It happened almost too quickly to notice. I knew that thought was not mine. It came from an outside source and not from my personal thoughts. It was *in* my thoughts, but it did not originate there. You know how I knew that? Because I didn't think Ken was a jerk, and, as a righteous child of God who is one in Christ, I do not generate evil thoughts or thoughts with an evil intention; these are suggestions presented to my mind, temptations coming from the Enemy. Once that lie became apparent to me, I spoke the truth and said out loud, "No he isn't!" and the Enemy moved on to his next strategy. In retrospect, I know that Lord was teaching me an important lesson that day; however, it doesn't mean I'm always on top of it. I have moments when I give into the temptation and fall for the Evil One's strategy.

As a counselor, I can't help but think how people's lives and relationships could be strengthened and they could become more productive if they understood this concept. I can't tell you how many couples I meet with who say and believe every thought that comes to their mind. Those words are destructive and damaging, but they would be a lot less damaging if the hearer remembered that the person doesn't mean what they are saying. It's coming from their mouth, but the source of it is not their spouse (or child, or parent, or friend) if they are in Christ and have His nature. If believers understood this, those hurtful words could be intercepted and left unspoken, knowing that it's not at all what they believe. The Enemy plants a thought in our mind that stirs up a feeling. That feeling is attached to some lie we've believed our whole life, and that lie will lead a person to do the very thing they do not wish. Paul explains this in the seventh chapter of Romans. When I'm angry with or hurt by someone, those feelings lead me to emotional reactions that become the perfect opportunity for the Enemy. He wants me to believe that what I'm feeling is true. He's got a whole script outlined for every scenario of my life. Here's a perfect example of something that used to happen in my marriage, until I recognized how the Enemy was at work:

Ken comes home late for dinner and forgets to call his wife Yolanda to let her know. He's done this many times in the past. Yolanda's problem is that she grew up believing that she wasn't important or loved because of events from her childhood that made her feel unworthy of being loved.

Yolanda notices the clock, which reads 6:45 PM and she begins to get angry since, as a small child, Yolanda learned to interpret the events and circumstances in her life through her feelings and whatever thoughts entered her mind. Consequently, she grew up with the belief that people didn't love her or think that she was important, and every time she felt that way, she believed it was true.

Yolanda learned to cope with the feelings of being unloved and worthless by withdrawing, feeling sorry for herself, and getting depressed. This was her fleshly reaction. As those around her paid attention to her, expressed concern about her depressed state, the depression became a covert way to get others to make her feel loved and important.

The Enemy's objective is to get Yolanda to draw life from getting her needs met her own way (her flesh) instead of from Jesus where she could experience victory in believing the truth of who she really is rather than how she feels.

Now it's 7:05 and Ken walks through the door. Before he can explain about the accident on the highway, Yolanda turns on her heels and retreats into her world of depression (her way of getting Ken to pay attention and make her feel loved and important, her flesh).

Does this illustration seem familiar to you? The Enemy knows what you believe about yourself, God, and others; and the thoughts that he presents to your mind, through *the power of sin,* will trigger the negative feelings and old beliefs which, in turn, lead you to your fleshly reactions.

Before we even think about walking according to our flesh, the power of sin is at work, placing thoughts into our minds that generate feelings that trigger a misbelief and, before you know it, we are living independently of Messiah in a desperate attempt to get something we believe we need. In reality, we are simply reacting to feelings that are attached to the lies we've believed all our lives that we must now purposefully replace with the truth.

If I have struggled with feelings of inferiority or inadequacy, *the power of sin* is going to tempt me with thoughts like, *Nothing I do is right* or *I need to be right* or *I'm a failure.* Then I will look to my flesh; perhaps compare myself to others, try harder, blame, argue, get angry or depressed, or be critical and judgmental in an effort to make myself *feel* better.

The Bible uses the term *power of sin* or *law of sin* (depending on the translation), which is indwelling sin. This is the sin that we all inherited from being born from Adam. This sin is not a verb but a noun, and it becomes the tool that the Evil One uses to tempt us and lure us away from finding life in Jesus. *Sin* is the entity that presents these thoughts to our mind in ways that make it seem like it's us, yet it's not us.

We tend to see people and circumstances that we are

unable to control as the problem when the real problem is what we believe about those people and circumstances because of the Evil One's work in our lives distorting truth. Remember, he is the Deceiver and we are the targets of his deception. The only freedom we have from this trap is what Jesus said in John 8:32, "You shall know the truth, and the truth will make you free."

5

VALLEY DUTY

Character cannot be developed in ease and quiet. Only through experience of trial and suffering can the soul be strengthened, ambition inspired, and success achieved.

—Helen Keller

I've often heard people say that when you first become a Christian, having placed your faith in Jesus, there is a honeymoon period. You know what I mean, a period of time when everything is wonderful, and you can't even fathom life taking a downward turn. It's sort of a euphoric time when you are lured into believing that it's always going to be wonderful and peaceful. My friend Kathy tried to tell me differently, but I refused to believe that what I was experiencing in my journey with Jesus wasn't going to last.

Yes, I attributed that peace to my newfound faith and

my happy circumstances, but that was about to change. God was growing me, and it was time for my first valley duty. By the time Rachel was three years old, we started trying to have another baby. Who would ever think after two pregnancies that I would have any difficulty? Well, after a year of failed attempts, I went to the doctor and he put me in the infertility program at Maxwell AFB in Fort Worth, Texas. Ken was firing live shots, so we ruled out their being anything wrong with him. Rather, we learned that I had developed a secondary infertility caused by a hormonal imbalance from my last pregnancy and my reproductive equipment wasn't doing what it was supposed to do. Everyone I knew was praying for me—people laying hands on me, prophesying, giving me words from God (*Hey, I have a word for God!*), and recommending this healer and that remedy. It was ridiculous; not that I wish to discount anyone who has been helped by any of these things.

GETTING TO KNOW GOD

I continued with the infertility program for several years, until one day when yet another pregnancy test, after dozens of prior tests, came back negative like all the rest. I was done. I shook my fist up in the air at God and screamed at the top of my voice, "I HATE YOU!" Poor Ken didn't know what to do. Was God going to strike us dead with a bolt of lightning? He was probably thinking he should hide under the bed. But he was definitely not coming anywhere near me! I went to sleep that night sobbing my eyes out. I was still a young and immature believer and didn't understand what being in the valley was all about in the life of a believer. I was still getting to know, really know, this God I loved deep down inside. But I didn't yet understand that valley duty is a necessary part of the believer's life. Today, after more valley duty than I can even recall, I look back on these times as having been the most meaningful in my life. But as a young believer, that was a foreign concept. I was still placing God on a performance-based system: I trust, believe, and love God when He performs based on my personal expectations. I was confusing God with a genie in a bottle, Santa Claus, and Mary Poppins.

When everyone around you is getting pregnant, having baby showers, and giving birth to babies (not to mention those who were aborting their babies), I felt like I was being punished for my past; another huge misconception of God. I felt marginalized and forgotten by a God who had, until then, been there for me in everything. Infertility is a lonely experience, even in the Church, people say things, hurtful things, without realizing it; for example, "You already have a child, so just be happy with that," or "You can always adopt," or "You shouldn't get your identity from being a mom." I just wanted to punch someone in the nose, but I restrained myself! The Evil One was having a field day with me, filling my mind with all sorts of lies, like *God is punishing me because I had an abortion.*

Here was part of the problem for me: after the first year of trying to conceive without success, the Lord spoke very specifically to me where I happened to be reading in my Bible that day. He said that I would conceive and have a baby boy. The problem was, I assumed it would happen nine months later, but that wasn't what He planned, nor what He said.

One Sunday morning when we arrived at church, I felt a deep remorse when I realized that I had turned getting pregnant and having another child into an idol; it had become more important to me than God Himself, enough so that I cursed Him. During worship time, I cried and dropped to my knees (You could do that in this church!) and surrendered my idol to God.

After I surrendered this idol to God, I was truly at peace with not having another child, even willing to see God's promise remain unfulfilled, if that is what He should allow. I learned a lot about God and His character in this valley. My relationship with Him deepened and my ability to trust grew in proportion. This doesn't happen just from reading the Bible, doing Bible studies, and spending an hour in church on Sunday. It comes from experiencing the truth about God in the valleys where you meet Him face-to-face. You absolutely have to begin with the head knowledge and learn all about Him, but your faith and ability to trust Him isn't going to go anywhere if that's where you stay. I think our educational system and approach to learning proves that knowledge of the facts alone does not produce under-standing. It must be accompanied by experiential knowl-edge in order for its truth to stay with us throughout life. And further, we learn by repetition, not just by being exposed to something once or even twice. Paul refers to this as "renewing the mind" in Romans 12:2 where he discusses replacing old beliefs with new ones; in this case, truth: "And do not be conformed to this world, but be trans-formed by the renewing of your mind, so that you may prove what the will of God is, that which is good and acceptable and perfect" (Romans 12:2). When it came to trusting God and truly believing in His goodness, I was a slow learner, mostly because of how my concept of Him was formed based on my authority figures growing up.

I remember the time I bought a brand new shiny black Volkswagen Jetta. How I loved that car. One week, when

Ken was out of town on business, I was sharing carpool duty with another family. After I dropped the kids off at school, I stopped at our local hardware store and ran in to get something before I headed home. It was early in the morning and there weren't many cars in the parking lot. A couple of minutes later, as I came out of the store and approached my car, I noticed a three-inch dent in the upper fender on the driver's side. The paint was scraped off. There was a big truck parked next to me, however there wasn't any damage on the truck. My car didn't have so much as a scratch on it before I parked and went into the store, yet there was no way I could prove who made the dent. I was furious, not to mention sick to my stomach, and filled with dread at telling Ken what happened. Between the kids and me, all he ever heard was, "It's not my fault." I climbed into the car and on my way home I heard the Lord speaking to me to just let it go. It's only a car; don't let it ruin your day. He told me to just give it to Him and trust Him, which is exactly what I did.

My car stayed in the garage all day, until it was time for me to pick up the kids from school. As soon as they saw the dent, they asked me what happened. When we got home, I parked the car in the garage and went about my business until that evening when Ken arrived home from his trip. When I told him what happened, he calmly went out to the garage to see the damage. About five seconds later, he came back in and said, "I don't see anything. Can you come show me?" So, I'm thinking this is like any man who opens the refrigerator to get the milk, and not seeing what's right in front of him! I'm a little annoyed now that I have to come downstairs and show him the damage when even Stevie Wonder could find it. Just as I started to point out the damage to him, I couldn't believe what I was seeing. I started screaming and crying, "It's gone, it's gone!" Ken just looked at me and told me to stop playing around, something we often did. As he was laughing at me, I ran into the house to get my eyewitnesses. Rachel, who was about fifteen years old at the time and also annoyed that her father couldn't see the dent, pointed to the place where it had been and started screaming, "Mom, what happened? Where's the dent?"

There we were, completely dumbfounded and in utter amazement because the dent was completely gone and, not only that, the paint was perfect! *Give it to Me, Yolanda and trust Me,* is what the Lord said. Ken too was amazed. I told this story to more people than I could count and the only person who didn't believe me was my brother, the atheist.

EXPERIENCING GOD

God was teaching me a lesson that would stay with me for all of my days. A lesson about trust, about listening to His voice and about His faithfulness. Do you think that a stupid dent on a Jetta really matters in the scheme of things? No. That dent was like a broken eyelash compared to all the really big stuff going on around us, but God wanted me to know that I mattered to Him. You'd think I would get the concept there and then, but I'm sorry to say that, though the foundation was laid, it was a lesson I would continue to learn by sheer repetition.

I got to know God in the valleys. When I think about David, the psalmist, and his relationship with God, his intimacy with Him was obvious to me. It was an intimacy born out of his times in valleys. Many of David's trials were due to his own poor choices, but in all of them, he sought God.

The LORD is my shepherd,
I shall not want.
He makes me lie down in green pastures;
He leads me beside quiet waters.
He restores my soul;
He guides me in the paths of righteousness for His
name's sake.
Even though I walk through the valley of the shadow of
death, I fear no evil, for You are with me;
Your rod and Your staff, they comfort me.
You prepare a table before me in the presence of my
enemies;
You have anointed my head with oil;
My cup overflows.
Surely goodness and lovingkindness will follow me
all the days of my life,
And I will dwell in the house of the LORD forever.
(Psalm 23, emphasis added)

David wrote about a God who was *with* us. No matter what we face in life, we have no reason to fear because God is with us. But there's more! As new covenant saints, we have God *in* us. With this reality, we have nothing to fear. In every valley we walk through, we walk with Jesus *in* us and *we* in Him. Jesus Himself is the rod and staff that comforts us; the same staff that Moses lifted up in the Wilderness and at the edge the Red Sea! And He will provide for us in that valley whatever He knows we need.

The Psalms, and particularly the ones penned by David, "a man after God's own heart," provide a backdrop and a glimpse into the heart of God and His children. They comfort and instruct, lament, and inspire; bless and curse. David's Psalms praise, plead, instruct, reflect, recount, and correct. In tone, they span the gamut of every human emotion from ecstasy to despair, indignation to remorse, grief to relief, fear to awe, and rage to love. They speak to us about the benefits of righteousness, the pitfalls of evil, the grandeur of the universe, and the corruption of mankind. In metaphors and poetry unsurpassed, the psalms depict God's might, His benevolence, His judgment, His compassion, His mercy, and His glory. David could only write about these things, because he experienced them in some of the darkest valleys of his life. It was there that he didn't just learn about God, but experienced God and came to *know* Him in an intimate way, the way you and I are now challenged to know Him. Here are a few references to some of David's valleys:

- Saul sent men to watch David's house and kill him (Psalm 59, 1 Samuel 19:11)
- He fled to Gath (Psalm 56, 1 Samuel 21:10)
- He pretended to be insane (Psalm 34, 1 Samuel 21:13)
- He escaped to the cave of Adullam (Psalm 142, 1 Samuel 22:1)
- Doeg the Edomite informed Saul of David's location (Psalm 52, 1 Samuel 22:9)
- The Ziphites betrayed David to Saul (Psalm 54, 1 Samuel 23:19)
- He hid from Saul in a cave (Psalm 57, 1 Samuel 24:1)
- He spared Saul (Psalm 18, 1 Samuel 24:11-2)
- He received forgiveness for his sin with Bathsheba (Psalm 32, 2 Samuel 12:13-14)
- He confessed his lustful and deceitful sin with Bathsheba (Psalm 51, 2 Samuel 12:13-14)

- He fled from Absalom (Psalm 3, 2 Samuel 15:14-16)
- Ziba refreshed David and his men (Psalm 63, 2 Samuel 16:2)

David's litany of woes is endless. It seems that David was always on the run from someone who was out to get him. King Saul wanted him dead and so did the Philistines, the Moabites, and the Ammonites. He had plenty of family problems too: His son Amnon raped his daughter Tamar, His son Absalom murdered his brother Amnon and then commits treason by trying to usurp David's throne, and David's child with Bathsheba dies. I think it's safe to say that David was a Valley Guy. The Psalms are rich with the lessons he learned there and are a chronicle of a faith in God, borne out of those valleys.

Perhaps you are like I was, a young and inexperienced believer starting out on your journey with Jesus and you can't imagine why those valleys are necessary, or you think they can somehow be averted by your careful obedience and forethought. There's not much point in my telling you what Kathy tried to tell me; you would just have to find out for yourself. The road to the deeper things of God doesn't lead to the mountaintops, it leads to the valleys and God will take you there because that's what love does. He loves you too much to leave you to your own devices, plans, and shortcuts.

6

THE VALLEY REVISITED

Hope deferred makes the heart sick but desire fulfilled
is a tree of life.

—Proverbs 13:12

I learned some important lessons in my first visit to the valley. I came face-to-face with my own fleshly need to control God. If you don't really believe on a heart level that He's good, that He's faithful, that He's loving and personal, and has your best interests at heart; then you're going to resort to control tactics when things don't go your way. It's just like when you were three years old and you didn't want to go to bed. Even as a three-year-old, you had a well-honed strategy for avoiding bedtime—you claimed you were thirsty or still hungry or not sleepy, you asked for a bedtime story and when it was over, you asked for another, then another. Get my point? Maybe your mom was controlled by your need to get your way, but God isn't. He isn't terribly moved by our discomfort, particularly when removing it conflicts with His best for us. That's not to say He isn't sympathetic or compassionate, but He just isn't a reactor. He watched His own Son suffer and die on a cross, right?

My infertility experience and all the valleys that followed have taught me in an *experiential* way what is really true about God. Yes, I learned all about God's nature and character by studying the Scriptures, but that was merely information that I learned on an *intellectual* level. It has been the valley *experiences* that have taught me on a heart-level, which is where information is translated into conviction and belief. If what we know on an intellectual level doesn't make its way into our belief system through our experience with Him, then we will never really trust Him. Consequently, avoiding those valley experiences (as if we could) wouldn't serve us well, since they're crucial to our spiritual formation and growth. Granted, they aren't much fun, and no one enjoys being there. To be honest, I can be a whiner when I'm going through a difficult time. In the moment, God seems to be nowhere in sight but, in retrospect, I see all the benefits and the fruit produced during that time.

We were living in Texas when Ken received orders for his next assignment. Off we went on our new adventure— to live one hour north of London by train and just fifteen minutes west of Cambridge. We arrived in May of 1987 and it took no time for England to capture my heart. I loved everything about it—the thatched-roof houses, the scones with clotted cream and Earl Grey tea, the famous Underground, and the trains (so many trains!). Then there were the endless fields of sheep dotting the countryside (I try not to think about them on my dining room table for dinner). There were the castles, the museums, the shopping, and the royals. There was the ferry from England to The Continent, before there was the Eurostar. And last but not least, there was London theatre (except when we sat in "the gods," as they call the seats so high up that you need binoculars). I loved it all, even though I had to endure living without a garbage disposal or air conditioning for three years!

GOD KEEPS HIS PROMISES

The only damper on life in England was the ongoing hormonal imbalance causing my infertility. I felt bad for Ken and now-seven-year-old Rachel having to deal with my out-of-control mood swings. I had become a cross between Dr. Jekyll and Mr. Hyde, and maybe one of those raptors from Jurassic Park thrown into the mix. I woke up one morning praying and asking God to heal me from this imbalance just so I could be normal again and not this crazy person. After I prayed, I opened my Bible as usual to read where I'd left off. The Lord spoke to me when my eyes landed on Psalm 84:11, "No good thing will I withhold from those who walk uprightly." I made a note in the margin with the date and went about my business. *Nah*, I thought, *it doesn't mean anything*, still doubting God.

Several weeks later, Aunt Flo didn't come, and I was never late. I waited another week. Still nothing. I bought a home pregnancy test, and, to my complete surprise, it was positive. Of course, I didn't believe it. Wasn't I infertile? I made an appointment with my physician at the Air Force Base who did another pregnancy test and when she announced, "Mrs. Stith, your test was positive. You're pregnant," I sat in her office with tears of joy running down my cheeks. *God, you kept your promise!* Look at some of these promises of God:

- All that the Father gives Me will come to Me, and the one who comes to Me I will certainly not cast out. (John 6:37)
- For I am convinced that neither death nor life, neither angels nor demons, neither the present nor the future, nor any powers, neither height nor depth, nor anything else in all creation, will be able to separate us from the love of God that is in Christ Jesus Our Lord. (Romans 8:38-39)
- He made Him who knew no sin to *be sin* on our behalf, so that we might become the righteousness of God in Him. (2 Corinthians 5:21)
- But if any of you lacks wisdom, let him ask of God, who gives to all generously and without reproach, and it will be given to him (James 1:5)
- For I know the plans I have for you," declares the Lord, "plans to prosper you and not to harm you, plans to give you a hope and a future. (Jeremiah 29:11)
- And my God will meet all your needs according to the riches of His glory in Christ Jesus. (Philippians 4:19)
- And we know that God works all things together for good to those who love God, to those who are called according to His purpose. (Romans 8:28)

These verses only scratch the surface of God's promises to His children. The question is, do we believe them? Do we believe that He's actively engaged in our lives, that He's personal, and that He cares about what we care about, even the trivial things, like parking spaces?

The hormone imbalance, the resulting infertility, and those mood swings built my faith in a God who never fails, who keeps His word and who is near to the brokenhearted. This was a huge lesson for me that would carry me through many more valleys, darker and more painful ones.

At the end of my first trimester I lost the baby. He died in utero and I had to be induced and go through a horrendous labor by myself in a British hospital to deliver the fetus. Now that I remember, there is one thing about England that I didn't like and that was their archaic form of practicing medicine, at least at the time, in the small town in Huntingdonshire.

The baby boy whom God promised me died and yet this did not shake my faith because in my valley, I had come to know Him as the God who never fails, the God who keeps His Word, and the God who is near to the broken-hearted. I don't believe that the baby I lost was, in fact, God's promised baby boy; but at the time, I didn't know that. I had no idea what the Lord was going to do. We never do, because He never tells. All I had was my trust in this faithful God whom I had come to know.

I carried this confidence in my heart. I knew God healed me from the hormone imbalance because, even though I lost the baby, I had been able to conceive when I wasn't even trying; so it would happen again in God's time. I was strengthened by His grace and the assurance that His promise to me wasn't *that* baby, but another one. It's important to note that I was not focused on getting pregnant again. Instead, God had filled me with "the peace that passes all understanding," that is, Jesus Himself. My relationship with Him was growing. I began to recognize that the pain in my life was the catalyst for me to know God and to find Him, not on the pinnacles of my life experiences, but in the darkest valleys.

Surprise, surprise! About six months later, I was pregnant again and on June 16, 1989, I gave birth to the boy that God promised. It was a rough delivery and, once again, I was in the hospital near our local village. After about twelve hours of labor, things weren't moving along like the medical team hoped, so they induced me. I had received an epidural to numb the pain but, after several hours, my uterus ruptured and the baby's heart rate dropped, or was it mine that dropped? I think it was both. He wasn't getting enough oxygen and I had turned as white as a sheet. I was rushed into surgery where my son was delivered by cesarean section. The epidural notwithstanding, I felt every bit of the pain when my uterus ruptured under the pressure of the labor.

We named our son Benjamin, which means *Son of the Right Hand*. In the Book of Genesis, Rachel gave birth to her last child, Benjamin. But at birth he had been called Ben-oni, which means *Son of Affliction*. Genesis 35:16-18 tells the story. "Then they journeyed from Bethel; and when there was still some distance to go to Ephrath, Rachel began to give birth and she suffered *severe labor*. And it came about when she was in severe labor that the midwife said to her, 'Do not fear, for now you have another son.' And it came about as her soul was departing (for she died), that she named him Ben-oni; but his father called him Benjamin, *Son of the Right Hand*." The *Son of Affliction* becomes the *Son of the Right Hand*. It is interesting to me that long before our son was even born, in *severe labor* as it turns out, we had chosen to name him Benjamin after my maternal grandfather. This proved to be prophetic in ways that we would eventually discover.

BE CAREFUL WHAT YOU PRAY FOR

Benjamin was not like his sister Rachel. She had been an easy baby who loved to eat and sleep. That girl slept through the night at six weeks old. Not Benjamin. He never slept through the night as a baby. He was a cheerful baby as long as he was being held and was interacting with us, but when we put him down to play or at bedtime, he wailed. And wailed. This became the pattern for his first two years. Ken would have to come home from work early enough so I could cook dinner while he held Benjamin. We tried a swing, since Rachel loved that, but he wasn't having it. This boy took over our lives, as we tried desperately to comfort him.

In 1990, when Benjamin turned one, we left England and settled in Rockville, Maryland, where we spent the next three years. Then Ken received orders for an assignment at Hickam AFB in Honolulu. In that three-year period in Rockville, we had a wonderful support system with our faith community and friends. I didn't want to leave. It was the first place that felt like home to us. But off we went, with me kicking and screaming, to Paradise. Ben had just turned four when we finally found a house to rent on the windward side of the island in Kailua. I was miserable for the first nine months. Ken was the director of finance for the entire Pacific region which meant he traveled regularly to the Air Force bases in Korea, Japan; Okinawa, Alaska; and Washington State. That meant I was alone with a preteen and a four-year old who was out-of-control. Really, God? I'm sure there's a lesson in all of this, but I was so over Hawaii after the first three months. I didn't know anyone, and we hadn't yet found a place of worship that was right for us. A typical day for me was getting up in the morning and dodging the mosquitoes, geckos, and palmetto bugs (code for flying roaches); and trying to protect our cat from Ben giving her a haircut and chasing her with a curtain rod. Oh, and trying to keep him in bed at night, while the geckos dropped from the ceiling. I missed home and my friends and wondered why on earth God made us move to Paradise. I was sitting in the backyard reading one day, batting the mosquitoes while they were having their lunch, and Rachel came outside and asked point blank, "Mom, why did God give us Ben?" A reasonable question coming from a twelve-year-old who'd spent the past four years of her life watching this child usurp her position as supreme being, scream, cry, and remain unfazed by our attempts at discipline or comfort. Out of my mouth came, "Rachel, God doesn't give us what we want. He gives us what we need." *What? Who said that?* I had never heard or thought that before, much less said it. But now, it became my mantra. It was profoundly true for me in my life. My son has been the single most important catalyst for growth in my journey with Jesus.

I prayed that the Lord would lead us to a place of fellowship and worship in Honolulu and He did, but not on the town side of Hawaii. Nonetheless, Kailua Community Church was a gift from God to us. It was a diverse community of believers—military families, retirees, locals, and all colors of the rainbow. They embraced us and we were at home, at least for now. They were hugely supportive of Israel and the Jewish people. They even celebrated Passover and Sukkot (Feast of Tabernacles) with our family. We taught them Israeli dances and Ken became an elder and served as their worship leader. That church was a demonstration of God's grace and an oasis for me during a time of loneliness and separation from family and friends on the mainland.

Things with Benjamin were getting progressively more difficult. Now he was in kindergarten and teachers were struggling with him. I was certain that he had ADHD, but Ken didn't want to believe that. Denial was often the way he coped with unpleasant things in our lives, simply pretending it wasn't an issue. Sure, easy for him to do, since he was traveling all the time for work. However, he finally agreed to our taking Benjamin to the military base hospital for an evaluation. Unfortunately, our plan was interrupted. In the middle of all the red tape, the Air Force scheduled us to leave Hawaii. At that point, Ken decided to retire from the military and begin a civilian career back on the mainland.

Leaving Hawaii was bittersweet, since we had come to love our friends and church; but on the other hand, I was thrilled to move back to the DC area, to buy a home, and establish permanent roots. See ya, mosquitoes, geckos, and, yeah, flying roaches! Oh, wait, we have mosquitoes in DC too. Nothing is perfect.

LOSING CONFIDENCE IN MYSELF

My journey of brokenness continued once we were back in Rockville. I'm talking about the kind of brokenness that the Apostle Paul meant in his letter to the Philippians:

We are the true circumcision [children of God or believers], who worship in the Spirit of God and glory in Christ Jesus and put no confidence in the flesh, although I myself might have confidence even in the flesh. If anyone else has a mind to put confidence in the flesh, I far more: circumcised the eighth day, of the nation of Israel, of the tribe of Benjamin, a Hebrew of Hebrews; as to the Law, a Pharisee; as to zeal, a persecutor of the church; as to the righteousness which is in the Law, found blameless. But whatever things were gain to me, those things I have counted as loss for the sake of Christ. More than that, I count all things to be loss in view of the surpassing value of knowing Christ Jesus my Lord, for whom I have suffered the loss of all things, and count them but rubbish in order that I may gain Christ, and may be found in Him, not having a righteousness of my own derived from the Law, but that which is through faith in Christ, the righteousness which comes from God on the basis of faith. (Philippians 3:3-9)

There is a lot to say about this passage in Philippians, but let me begin by pointing out the main issue at hand in this passage. There is one word that Paul uses three times in this passage, and when a Jewish person keeps repeating something, it's because it's the key to what he's talking about. The word is *confidence*. Paul never actually uses the word *broken* to describe himself in this passage, does he? But what he does make apparent is that he had a *confidence* problem. Where did Paul place his confidence as a religious person? The passage tells us: he placed it in his pedigree as a Jewish man, and not just any Jewish man, but a student of the Law. He placed his confidence in his performance as one who lived what the Law called a righteous life, and he even condemned those who did not. However, in light of the cross and the righteousness that came to him on the basis of his faith in Jesus, he considered all his earlier confidences as worthless, counting them as useless in order to know his Messiah. It wasn't that God was breaking *Paul*. He was breaking Paul's *confidence* in his own self-sufficiency, his own abilities and his own performance, so that he could find his life in Jesus and not in the Law. Paul writes:

For we do not want you to be unaware brethren, of our affliction which came to us in Asia, that we were *burdened excessively, beyond our strength,* so that we despaired even of life; indeed, we had the sentence of death within ourselves in order that we should not trust in ourselves, but in God who raised the dead. (2 Corinthians 1:8-9, emphasis added)

It's very simple. Brokenness is a state of being in which we lose confidence in living life apart from Messiah and, instead, our suffering and afflictions—our valleys—become our classroom.

7

WHEN THE WHEELS FALL OFF
THE BUS

Let me tell you the one thing I have against Moses. He took us forty years into the desert in order to bring us to the one place in the Middle East that has no oil!

—Golda Meir

*a*s you know by now, the death of my husband was not my first valley experience. No, I wasn't a novice when it came to trials and difficulties, but the valleys I walked through prior to Ken's death certainly prepared me for it; sort of like spiritual boot camp. When Ken graduated from college through ROTC, off he went to the Air Force version of boot camp on Martha's Vineyard. Ken was no dummy! Of course, the other three armed service branches just make fun of those guys, but I'm thinking that he who laughs last, laughs best. Twice in my adult life I got talked into going camping with a group of girlfriends. After that? No thank you. Not for me. For one thing, it's dirty. Then there's the insect and wildlife population, not to mention the inevitable downpour. Camping for this Jewish-American princess is staying at a Holiday Inn instead of the Hyatt Regency. My people spent four hundred years in the wilderness and, since then, Jews don't camp! Well, apparently, neither do African Americans, much for the same reason.

God's boot camp might not have all the physical hardship I just described, but it sure as heck has emotional hardship and I've already tasted what that's like. The problem is, I had very little understanding that boot camp, both the military kind and God's, is about developing people.

SELF-SUFFICIENCY

In the mid-1990s, I hit a wall in my walk with the Lord. I didn't know it at the time, but I had a problem. I only knew that my life was no longer working the way I had always approached it. The wheels were falling off my bus. I had been the go-to girl, the person who appeared to have everything under control; the one who knew all the answers. It didn't matter what the questions were! If I didn't know the answer, I'd BS my way through to give one. People would come to me and depend on me for . . . well, just fill in the blank. The fact that I had no boundaries only made me a target for becoming a professional "rescuer" and "helper." As someone who was naturally compassionate and sympathetic, I was always willing to do whatever was needed at the moment. I would have been considered a giving person, but I later discovered not all of my giving was selfless.

Now back in Rockville, Maryland, following Ken's retirement from the Air Force, he took a civilian job and we bought a house that would accommodate my aging parents moving from LA and living with us. Isn't that what a good daughter does? A daughter who loves God and wants to bless and honor her parents? Isn't that what you do if you're a good Christian? At this time, I was losing two friends. My best friend was moving all the way to Alaska to go to Bible school and my other best friend was dying from two terminal illnesses and I had been deeply involved in her care. Oh, and I almost forgot to mention the surfacing of some teenage rebellion coming from Rachel at the time. My human resources were being removed from me one by one and, at the same time, the pressures of life were ramping up. It was the perfect storm, the result of my misguided choice (motivated by wrong thinking with good intentions) and circumstances (the loss of my human resources) that I could not control. God had His fingerprints all over it.

LOSING STEAM

After nine months of my parents living with us, Mom and Dad and I assumed our old roles, reverting to unhealthy behaviors, and with everything else going on, I wanted out as fast as I could. Not only were the wheels falling off my bus, but the engine was dying a slow death. I didn't know it then, but I soon discovered that all my "helping" and "rescuing" was motivated by a deep need in me to be loved and wanted and to feel a sense of adequacy, which was completely absent from my childhood experience. I confided in no one until I finally reached out to my congregational leader at the Messianic congregation we attended. I needed help. He told me about a ministry that provided faith-based, Jesus-centered counseling that would help. "Yolanda," he said, "you just need a couple of sessions and then you'll be fine." Ha! Was he ever wrong! I can't blame him though; I was a pretty good performer and had everyone fooled, including myself.

It took a lot for me to admit I had a problem, but that only tells you just how bad things were because everything in my life was spinning out of control. The counseling proved to be divine providence and in a short amount of time, although not just a couple of sessions, I felt like a new person even though the circumstances in my life had not changed. In fact, they got progressively worse.

THE EXCHANGED LIFE

After I completed counseling at Grace Ministries, I was encouraged to sign up for their discipleship counseling training program. This was God opening a door for me. Once I completed all the training and underwent an intensive internship, I was eventually invited to become a staff counselor at this ministry.

The counseling and training I received at Grace Ministries (GM) changed my life forever. I learned that my basic problem was self-sufficiency. I was living the Christian life, not by depending on the life of Jesus within; but by depending on my own resources—my self-confidence, capabilities and achievements—in an effort to gain people's approval and maintain God's blessings in my life. Like Paul, I had a confidence problem. I knew that I couldn't earn my eternal salvation or get my sins forgiven any other way except by grace through faith (Ephesians 2:8-9), but I was definitely relying on myself to earn God's blessings by living a righteous life. Living life this way was exhausting and since I was very much a doer, I did it to the hilt. I did it by reading my Bible and praying daily for an hour and a half. I did it by serving in my local congregation as children's ministry leader, women's ministry leader, and Israeli dance ministry leader, just to name a few. Oh, and by sharing my faith with anyone who had a pulse. All this kept me on a perpetual religious performance treadmill. I was hard-wired for self-discipline and staying busy filled my emotional tank. God managed to use me in these ministries, but I didn't realize I was coming to the end of myself—the best place for me to be.

When we place our faith in Christ, we don't immediately begin living as though our faith is in Him. Faith is a gift that we receive, and we all get the same amount of faith (Romans 12:3). However, our faith must grow in order for us to live the life that we now have within us. Paul says in Galatians 2:20 "I have been crucified with Christ and it is no longer I who lives, but Christ lives in me; and the life which I now live in the flesh I live by faith in the Son of God, who loved me and gave Himself up for me." This is the Exchanged Life—our old life, the life we were born into through Adam is exchanged for Jesus' life for the express purpose of living His life through us!

Through books that God brought across my path and through my counseling and training at GM, I discovered, or rather, God revealed to me, what the Christian life was about. It wasn't about me living *for* God, doing good works and following the rules; it was about Jesus *in* me living *through* me. The problem is that if you are not taught this truth, you will approach the Christian life through religious activity and performance and that was my conundrum.

I remember one day my counselor talking to me about the difference between living under The Law and living under grace. Until then, I never gave this dichotomy much thought, but then she challenged me to *not* read my Bible for one month. Are you kidding? Not read my Bible for a month? At all? I was filled with fear at the thought. But she was very wise. She asked me what was difficult about that for me. I told her that I believed if I didn't read my Bible and pray every day, something bad would happen; God would not bless me. As I write this, I am amused at how obsessive-compulsive I was back then, not to mention legalistic. Reluctantly, I agreed to the plan.

The first week without my Bible was hard. I was fearful and anxious, expecting something awful to happen. It was the same in week two. Each week I would report my experience to my counselor, and she would patiently listen and encourage me to continue with the plan. By week three, I began to notice something happening in my relationship with the Lord. Without any Bible study whatsoever, I became much more aware of God's presence and my connection with Him than ever before. What was once regimented to my hour and half every morning was now an intimate communion that I enjoyed throughout my day and into the night. At the end of week four, I told my counselor that my time with the Lord was more meaningful than it had ever been just by talking with Him and listening to Him throughout the four weeks. While I resumed my morning reading and prayer, it was no longer motivated by fear, but by "delighting myself in the Lord." If for some reason I don't read my Bible on a particular day, I know I'm safe and secure in Him, and that my security, well-being, and blessings are freely given in Messiah and not contingent upon my self-disciplined behavior. This was a great lesson for me.

I remained a staff discipleship counselor at Grace Ministries for seventeen years. After the first year, I took over as director of training. I probably learned just as much

as a counselor and teacher as I did when I was in counseling myself, since God was forever opening my eyes to
aspects of my life that I still had not surrendered fully to
Him. A year after I started at GM, Ken went through their
training and also joined the staff as a part-time volunteer,
counseling men and participating in the training.

In 2014, the Lord made it very clear to us that it was
time to move on. He had been trying to get my attention for
at least a year about leaving GM, but I found great security
in what I was doing. To be honest with you, I could do my
job in my sleep and I was no longer being challenged.
When God wants your attention, He knows just how to get
it and so Ken and I knew in our hearts it was time to leave.
But we were leaving to do what? That was the big question
and, of course, God wasn't telling us. All I knew was that
He wanted us to trust Him and make the decision to go and
everything else would fall into place in due time.

After leaving Grace Ministries, Ken and I prayed for
God's direction and He put it on our hearts to start our own
counseling ministry. He gave Ken the name New Heart
Living, and before we knew it, we had a board of directors,
our non-profit status, and plenty of clients. New Heart
Living (NHL) was a huge leap of faith for us, one that I
would never have taken on my own and, of course, God
knew that. He also knew that Ken was not going to be there
long, and He wanted to leave me with something that
would give me a reason to keep going and using the gifts
He'd given me. In hindsight, it all makes perfect sense but,
at the time, it was a step of faith not knowing what God
was up to, even though we knew He was leading us in this
direction. Really, do we ever know what God is doing or
why? This life is just one big surprise party and wild
adventure.

Everything I learned at GM, and that we teach at NHL, has prepared me for this valley I am currently walking through, grieving the loss of my husband as well as my former life as a married woman and some friends that were dear to me.

When the dust settled and the reality set in that this nightmare was not going to end after a couple of weeks or even months, I got back to work, because I figured what I needed the most was hearing God's truth—the truth about a faithful, loving and merciful God and the truth that my identity is in Jesus and not my marital status—and the best way for me was counseling and teaching it. Was it a coincidence that, suddenly, I was getting more and more clients who were grieving loss? And so, as I helped clients walk through their Valley of Achor, God walked me through mine.

So many of my clients wrestle with their concept of God, especially when they have encountered circumstances in life that have left them wondering if He was there in the first place. And if He was there, how could He stand by and allow such things to happen? How is it that a loving God allows a five-year old boy to die in a car crash by a drunk driver? If God is sovereign, then why does He allow a young man barely out of his youth to lose three of his limbs, his own personal faith, and his best friend who died serving his country on a battlefield in Afghanistan? Where is God when a young child is repeatedly molested in his home by family members and Mom and Dad do nothing to protect him? God's love and sovereignty in a world of suffering makes for interesting conversation. I certainly do not profess to have all the answers, but what I know is that while God is love and is sovereign, He created man with a free will, the ability to make his own choices, to accept

God's love or reject it. If God were to take away man's free will, man would be reduced to a human robot functioning on command, as opposed to living life with conscious volition. Consequently, lacking free will, man would never be able to experience authentic love. God created man out of His desire to bestow His extravagant love upon him and share with him an intimate and eternal relationship. And I'm here to tell you, that the more loss you've experienced in your life and the more pain you've suffered, the deeper that intimacy will be between you and God—if you seek him there.

In addition, while we know God is sovereign—that He is God, the Supreme Being, Ruler of all, the Creator of the universe and everything in it—that does not mean He controls His creation, particularly since He created man to have the freedom to make his own choices. What kind of God says, "I made you to have a free will for a reason, but I'm going to interfere and take away your free will, because I'm God and I can"? That's illogical! He is not going to go against His own reasoning and wisdom when it comes to His creation.

I have to admit that I don't understand why such horrible things happen to some and not to others, but I do know that the *whys* in life are only for God to know and I am not God. I cannot know what He knows and see what He sees. Therefore, I must conclude that everything that happens may not necessarily happen for a good reason. But God, who is the supreme force for good in this world, will absolutely make something good of it if we invite Him into the tragedy and chaos of our lives.

The critical aspect of surviving valley life, even short stints, is being absolutely convinced of God's character. We must know that, regardless of outcomes, painful circumstances, situations out of our control, negative emotions, and erroneous thoughts; God is good and everything He's up to is good. I didn't just wake up one day and believe that about God. It has become a conviction of mine based on forty years of valley experiences and God's provision of Himself in those valleys.

God has taught me, through perseverance and trust that He is good. Now here's the problem for most folks: they define "good" as something they like and that *feels* good, but God does not. What we call "good," God often calls "not good" and vice versa. Who would say it was good that an innocent man should die for the guilty?

Coming to the end of one's own ways of living—managing, balancing, and controlling—must go hand in hand with faith in a God that transcends the things of this world and hopes in and trusts the God of all creation. We won't necessarily understand everything about Him, nor will we be able to make sense of the pain and suffering in this world; we only need to believe that He is good. Always.

8

THE NEED FOR GOD

In the book of life, the answers are not in the back.

—Charlie Brown

*I*n case you haven't noticed, I can be pretty sarcastic, even sardonic, at times. Some people don't respond well to it and sort of look at me with an incredulous "Is she joking or what?" kind of look. If I'm in the South, I might get that condescending "bless her heart" kind of look. In surviving, perhaps even thriving, in our valleys, we need humor. If you can't find the humor in life, even in the bad times, then you're in big trouble. Oh, maybe you won't be able to laugh initially, but after you've processed and recalculated your mind-set to your current reality, having the ability to laugh is cathartic, and the darker the humor the better, I say!

When things start heating up or it looks like the sun is

about to set on your current status-quo, you know that you're about to go through something hard. Like me, you may begin chasing after the sun as if to prevent it from going down. But someone once said that we need to do the opposite and run toward the dark because the next sunrise is just around the corner.

Do you ever feel like God is picking on you or that there's something so fundamentally messed up about you, that you've become God's special project? Honestly, there were times I felt that way, even though I knew intellectually it wasn't true. In my twisted humor, I would whine, *Lord, why don't you go pick on someone else for a while?* How glad am I that He has a sense of humor too and doesn't take what I say personally! I'm pretty certain that I was not alone in having a picture of God as a cosmic meanie. We might not even be consciously aware of it, much less speak it out loud to anyone. My thinking was that He had his favorites, but then there are others, like me, whom He picked on. Mind you, this was a subconscious belief of mine. On an intellectual level, where I am conscious of what I think based on God's Word, I didn't believe that. It is in our core, deep in the subconscious mind that we house all the erroneous beliefs and lies that stem from our history. I know this to be true, because whenever bad things happened, God was the first person I blamed. When God didn't answer my prayers according to my expectations, I would get angry with Him and *feel* unloved and forgotten by Him. Was this true? Was I unloved and forgotten by Him? No, but it's what I believed deep down and that was the problem.

As someone with big emotions, I spent my life relying on my internal barometer to evaluate and determine what's true. So if I felt a certain way, it was a losing battle for me to avoid letting that emotion control me. Most of us fall into one of two groups: feelers or thinkers; and even though both feeling and thinking are necessary and unavoidable, we can't rely on them to tell us what's true; only God can do that. He not only knows the truth, He is the Truth. Further, God's Word remains true, whether we feel it or think it or not. A relationship with God is based solely on faith. And faith is not dependent upon feelings or intellect, which are changeable or fallacious, but on what God says to be true. When we act on that, we get to experience the reality of that truth.

OUR CONCEPT OF GOD

For many years, my relationship with God was impeded by conflicting thoughts and feelings about Him that I knew were linked to my parents; specifically, my earthly dad. My dad and I did not have a good relationship. I think it had a lot to do with the fact that I reminded my dad of himself. I have a lot of his negative traits and some positive ones, as well. When I was a small child, my dad worked all the time and the only interactions I remember having with him were on Sundays when he, my mom, and I would go visit my grandparents or go for a drive somewhere. As I got older, we had family dinners together, but my dad never communicated with me at the table, much less showed any interest in what I'd been doing. Dad listened to the Dodgers, Rams, or Lakers games on the radio during dinner, and then sat in front of his TV after dinner for the remainder of the night. He never helped me with my schoolwork. I later learned that he barely had a fifth grade education himself, but I didn't know that at the time. The only time he ever paid attention to me was when my mom told him to administer punishment. That's when he took off his belt. How do you think that might have affected my understanding and view of my heavenly dad?

I'm fortunate, because God ultimately healed my relationship with my dad, and I was able to enjoy a loving relationship with him, even if it was never quite what I wanted it to be. But I stopped expecting my earthly dad to be something he could not be. He could never be for me what my Father in Heaven *alone* can be. Consequently, I was free to love my dad because I didn't need something from him; Jesus was fulfilling my need. Even so, the little problem remained: how my earthly dad had affected my concept of God. Eventually, I began to see the connection between these feelings and the erroneous beliefs I had about God, which I knew were not true. My dad played favorites and I was not his; Rhoda was. My parents had her in their youth and she was quiet and easy. By the time I came along, my parents were in their late thirties and my dad was pretty tired and stressed by then, trying to make my mother happy (a formidable task) and making his fortune. He was undemonstrative with me, never affirming and never encouraging. He basically ignored me unless he was angry, then watch out! I became a casualty of what is called *transference*. Transference is a phenomenon by which someone unconsciously redirects their feelings about one person by projecting them on to another. In laymen's terms, my concept of God was shaped by what I felt and believed on a subconscious level about my earthly father. We all do this and don't even recognize it. When the chips are down and we are struggling, our concept of God, formed from our childhood experiences, kicks in. We desire to trust Him, but we don't and that is why.

DANGER AHEAD: DEEP WATERS

My concept of God continued to interfere with my ability to trust Him when I was challenged. When Ben was diagnosed with ADHD as a child and given medication, parenting him became easier. I wouldn't say it was a walk in the park, but it was better. By the time he turned fifteen, however, I noticed changes in him that began to escalate slowly over the next ten years. It started with porn and lying, then it graduated to stealing and smoking pot. I became increasingly alarmed at his behavior because I could see where it was headed, and I was afraid. Benjamin was always in trouble. I used to joke about it and say that he was going to grow up and have a prison ministry—on the inside. That statement ended up being prophetic. By the time he was nineteen, we had sent him to a fancy (and expensive!) all-boy's prep school three and a half hours away, and he was expelled for having pot in his possession. Then the drugs got more serious and the stealing and the pathological lying increased, so we kicked him out of our home. This became the Stith routine for the next several years. In and out, in and out, in and out, like that West Coast burger joint. One day, after three days of being out of the house he wanted to come home, but I told him he had to go to rehab and deal with his drug issue, which he did, reluctantly. That's where he met the Man. The Man was in a local gang and Ben was a sitting target—young, looking for an identity, and a feeling of belonging, lost and naïve. He was socially and mentally behind in his years. He was initiated into the gang and the criminal activity increased along with his drug use. His father and I had absolutely no idea what was going on. I thought I knew my son, but this was not Ben. After the rehab debacle, we sent him to a Christian boot camp in Texas—epic fail. Then he went into another rehab facility and saw more therapists. The more we tried to find the right kind of help for him, the worse things got. My husband and I were out of ideas, options, and money. We were up to our eyeballs in debt and languishing in the deepest valley yet. This Valley Girl was running out of steam and there were times when it felt like my prayers were empty words just hitting the ceiling. We prayed constantly and our friends and church family all fervently prayed for us and especially for Ben.

Let me just say, this child of mine did not fit the profile for addicts or criminals. He was smart and adorable, funny and creative. He had so many wonderful qualities and gifts that I just couldn't understand what went so terribly wrong.

One morning in late December, I was talking to the Lord about my despair concerning Ben, as usual; but instead of getting some encouragement from Him, the Lord told me that he was going to go to jail. I'm not a "the Lord told me" kind of a person, but when He's speaking to me about something, I usually know it's Him, even if I don't always listen. I wasn't really surprised, since I kind of knew that the Lord was trying to tell me this for a while. That was all He told me—nothing else. I began to prepare emotionally for what I feared would happen from the time he was very young. Two weeks later, I was at work and my husband called. Very quietly and calmly, he told me that Ben was arrested at our house and called his dad from jail. Surprisingly, I hung up and just carried on with my work, because the Lord had prepared me for this moment.

Ben was arrested for conspiracy to commit robbery and assault. In other words, it was Ben's spark of genius (being the wildly creative person I knew him to be) to set the kid up who was dealing drugs and rob him. Ben was never

violent, nor did he have a weapon. In his naïve and immature mind, he thought they would just take the drugs and
money and be off on their merry way. Of course, my son,
the genius, underestimated the Man.

That evening my son called home, and I spoke to him.
He was nineteen years old, but emotionally and mentally
about twelve. He was terrified and crying, begging for our
help. For the first time in his life, I said "No." I reminded
Ben of a conversation we'd had about a month before in
which I had warned him that God told me that he was
going to go to jail, and that if anything happened to him as
a result of his involvement in illegal activity, that his Dad
and I would not help him and he would be on his own. It
was hard as hell, but I knew I couldn't rescue him from this
no matter what the outcome might be. I had to surrender
my boy to God and trust Him to deal with Ben and change
his life. Otherwise, we would be doing this with him for the
rest of our lives, as many parents do.

I told Ben that he would be assigned a court-appointed
defender (she was absolutely useless, but God was still on
His throne), that we would not pay for an expensive, highly
recognized attorney. When he asked me how he would
survive, I said, "Son, you will need to turn to Jesus." We
ended our five minutes, and I spent the rest of the night
crying until I finally fell asleep. The next day Ben called me
and said, "Mom, I prayed and asked Jesus to forgive me
and take over my life. I'm going to be okay." That was
January 15, 2009.

I'm not going to defend my son, because he was
involved with gang members and living like a criminal. He
was found guilty of conspiracy and although he wasn't
armed, the Man was, and Ben was there. He ended up
taking the rap for a drug run and robbery that went very

wrong. One kid who was also with them made a deal with the DA and pinned it all on Ben, and that kid only got thirty days with probation. The Man who used his knife and broke the nineteen-year-old drug dealer's jaw disappeared, and someone had to pay the price. Ben, with no priors, was sentenced to eighteen months in the county jail, and I fell apart in that courtroom as they handcuffed my son and ushered him away. In a sense, when Ben was locked up, it felt like I was locked up.

Perhaps most people would think that we should have hired an attorney who would, most certainly, have gotten him off on probation and maybe thirty days in jail; but how would that help Ben? What would he have learned from his stupid choices? He would have learned like most kids that every time he messes up, Mom and Dad were ready to come to the rescue. He would have learned nothing that would help him change the trajectory of his life and we would have, unwittingly, helped him stay stuck in behaviors and a lifestyle that would eventually destroy him. I have counseled many parents about looking at the big picture and what they really want for their child. Did they want them to be dependent on THEM the rest of their lives or find God? It was that simple; not easy, but simple. Of course, it requires a parent to be willing for *anything* to happen—particularly the things they don't want to happen —and trust in the Lord.

THE GOD WHO KEEPS HIS WORD

My memory of the whole experience, from Ben's sentencing to all the drama throughout his jail time, continues to be a dark one for me. We visited him twice a week until he went to the pre-release center (PRC) after ten months served.

There he was able to work or go to school and, with good behavior, come home on house arrest to finish out his time. So when he finally got approved to go to the PRC, we were thrilled. After several months, he was given permission for house arrest and allowed to live at home. Until that time, he had been coming home on weekends only and going with us to church, which he loved. Ben always had a heart for God.

The day Ben was scheduled to be released to us, his supervisor was at our house installing all the necessary security equipment that would activate his ankle bracelet and track his every move. Ken had left for the PRC to pick Ben up. I was so excited that he would be out of that environment and away from criminals. Or so I thought. After about an hour and a half, Ken called home and said that Ben was just arrested for possessing contraband. He was immediately sent back to the county jail to finish his last six months of incarceration, plus an extra month for his infraction. I went berserk! I could not believe that God allowed this to happen. Are you kidding me, Lord? I have done nothing but pray for this kid (the kid you gave me!), without ceasing, for years and now this? I was so angry with God I couldn't see straight. I was more angry with God over this than I was when I was trying to get pregnant years before and couldn't! In that moment, I mentally slammed the gavel down on God and pronounced Him to a life sentence.

Remember my childhood concept of God? Yep. Those are exactly the beliefs that started being triggered in me. I laid in my bed for two days and cried. The Deceiver's fingerprints were all over this. It never fails to happen the moment we invite doubt and unbelief to take over. I didn't pray and I didn't talk to anyone except Ben when he was allowed to call. And then I remembered the truth about God. I remembered that He is good and everything He does is good, even if I don't understand it and even when my emotions are telling me something different. My son going back to jail to do an additional seven months was good, but only God knew why. So I surrendered PRC and jail and another seven months of Ben being locked up to the Lord, washed my face and praised His name; sort of like King David did after his child with Bathsheba died.

Before this happened, I warned Ben that if he ever went back to jail, I would not visit him again. He would just have to do his time and I would see him when he was released. Another hard decision, but I stuck to it for the whole seven months and so did Rachel and his dad. Ben called me every day, and over the course of his entire incarceration he went to all the chapels and Bible studies, read all the books I sent him, most of his Bible, the entire *Left Behind* series and his favorite book, *The Shack* by William Paul Young. God finally had my son's full attention and Ben was experiencing the Lord's presence within him at work in his life.

The day of Ben's release from jail finally came. It was August 2, 2010. I couldn't bring myself to go to the jail to get him, so Rachel went and brought him home. When that boy walk through the door, the door to my heart flung open and I felt free once again. He asked me to take him to the bank to open a checking account and run some errands with him. He said he needed to talk to me about something really important. While we sat in the parking lot of the bank, he said, "Mom, I want you to just listen to what I am about to tell you. And please don't react." *Oh, boy,* I thought, *this is not going to be good.*

It was only then that Ben told me the whole story about the Man and the gang, how he was initiated, and how he knew immediately afterward that he'd made the biggest mistake of his life. But it was too late. Once you're in a gang, there's no way out, except in a body bag and Ben knew that. Every time the Man called him to do something, Ben had to comply, or he was dead. Then he began to tell me what happened when he went back to jail after getting kicked out of the PRC. He told me he prayed and prayed for a way out of the gang. He was afraid, and afraid for all of us too, but then a miracle happened. When Ben was sent back to jail from the PRC, he ended up with a cellmate who just happened to be in the same gang. After some time, Ben developed a relationship with this gang member who liked Ben. He asked him, "What is a kid like you doing in this place and in this gang? You aren't like us." Ben had told him all about his family and upbringing and this guy could see an educated young kid from an upper-middle class, God-centered family who loved him; nothing like his own experience. Almost immediately, Ben confided in his cellmate that he wanted out of the gang but knew it was impossible. Well, of all the cellmates that Ben could have ended up with in a jail population of thousands, God paired my son with the highest-ranking gang member of the same gang! This guy (who shall remain nameless) told Ben that he could arrange for him to be uninitiated by having three gang members beat him to a bloody pulp for five straight minutes without any resistance. Once the beating was complete, Ben would be dead to them and free to leave the gang; they would never bother him again. Ben jumped on it, and the day and time were set, making sure they weren't caught by any guards and disciplined by getting thrown in the hole.

As my son told me this story, I suddenly knew exactly why he got caught with contraband at the PRC and why

God made sure he was sent back to jail. I had been so angry with God when it happened, because it seemed that He betrayed me, that He had forgotten me and ignored my prayers when, in fact, He was in the process of answering my prayers all along! The tears of humility and brokenness flooded my eyes and stung my face as they slowly tracked down my cheeks, leaving their mark. What had been a dark, lonely valley had been filled with the light of the glory of God. He was there all along. As I ran into the darkness and away from the setting sun, I ran into the sunrise. My childhood concept of Him, derived from my experiences with my earthly dad, once again, clouded my vision. However, when I remembered the truth about God, I chose to continue to trust Him with my son and the remainder of his jail sentence.

You know you're a Valley Girl or Guy when you look for Jesus in the valley and choose the truth. I always say that sometimes we find ourselves in situations in which we can't see where we are or where we are going, and we must remember that God is good. It's like flying an airplane in the middle of a terrible storm and everywhere we look it's dark and the view is obstructed by clouds so that we can't see anything. The pilot must rely on his instruments to fly. Well, Jesus is like our instrument panel, guiding us through the storms of life, when we don't know where we are or where we're going. We must place our *confidence* and total faith in our instrument panel and continue to fly till we find dawn.

BELONGING

As far back as I can remember, I was in search of "a place" where my heart would find its home. *Home,* the place where we feel we belong, where we are safe and secure. Yet, many have come to think of home as a scary place, a place of uncertainty and vulnerability and maybe even violence; but that's not home as God intended for us. Home is where our hearts are at rest. Home is in God. We tend to think of heaven as our home, since ultimately that's where we all long to be when our time comes; however, our home is not a destination, but an attitude; a frame of mind, and a reality that transcends space and time.

God created us to find our home in Him and when we do, we are fully satisfied and at peace, because we are designed by our Creator to be complete in Him. There is no one or no thing that can complete us. And no, it's not true what Tom Cruise said to Renée Zellweger in the movie *Jerry Maguire*: "You complete me." No one can complete us but God, through Jesus our Messiah.

We have a heart that needs God and that was created to beat in sync with His, but that capacity was lost in the Garden of Eden. God's heart and man's heart operated in tandem until that fateful day of temptation in the Garden. I love what Brennan Manning said in his book called *Ruthless Trust*, "The splendor of a human heart which trusts that it is loved gives God more pleasure than Westminster Cathedral, the Sistine Chapel, Beethoven's Ninth Symphony, Van Gogh's *Sunflowers*, the sight of ten thousand butterflies in flight or the scent of a million orchids in bloom." In reality, there is nothing that touches God's heart like the heart of man fully surrendered to Him. Man's heart was made to trust his Creator, but trust was broken and hearts were broken and *home* became an elusive dream.

From the moment we're born, our hearts are in search of something to fill it. What we don't know is that it is God. Some find Him early in life, some later and some never find

Him. I think a lot of that has to do with the Tree of the Knowledge of Good and Evil. If we go back to the beginning, God told Adam in Genesis 2:16-17, "From any tree of the garden you may eat freely; but from the tree of the knowledge of good and evil you shall not eat, for in the day that you eat from it you will surely die." There were plenty of other trees from which to eat in the garden, and there was the Tree of Life. It was just that one tree they couldn't eat from. Why? My thoughts are that this tree was not made for man, but only for God Himself. In order to eat from this tree, one would need to be all-knowing, and there is only One who is all-knowing. Even with all of our education and advancements, man is limited. We can never know what God alone knows; we can only know what God reveals and allows us to know. God can see and judge the heart of every man, but we cannot, although we try! And because God is all-knowing, He knew that Adam would eat from the tree. God knew everything that was to come, even before creation. There's no crystal ball that can do that for man!

We read in Chapter Three of Genesis about the serpent's dialogue with Eve. He's described as crafty. Some good synonyms for crafty are deceitful, sneaky, conniving, and—my personal favorite— cunning; all of which describe his modus operandi. The way the serpent was leading Eve was not necessarily with obviously evil thoughts or suggestions, but veiled half-truths with evil intentions, which is exactly how he's operated since. He starts out by putting the woman on the defensive, always a good strategy with your opponent. "Indeed, has God said, 'You shall not eat from any tree of the garden'?" (Genesis 3:1). Why do you suppose he questioned her? Perhaps, he was trying to create doubt in her mind. The woman said to the serpent, "From the fruit of the trees [many trees] of the garden we may eat; but from the fruit of the tree which is in the middle of the garden, God has said, 'You shall not eat from it or touch it, or you will die.'" (Genesis 3:2-3). I believe the woman was getting defensive and beginning to doubt God, because she added something that God never said. He never said they cannot touch the tree. Now, granted, it would be a little difficult to eat the fruit without touching it somehow, but God never said, "Don't touch."

Something else to consider about God's warning to the man, and now his wife, is that God never explained the concept of death to them. Until this point, death had never occurred in the garden. I'm not sure what the implications of that might be, but it's something to ponder. "The serpent said to the woman, 'You surely will not die! For God knows that in the day you eat from it your eyes will be opened, and you will be like God, knowing good and evil.'" (Genesis 3:4-5). The serpent challenges the woman and declares God to be a liar. Next come half-truths mixed with another lie: they can be "like" God. They can never be God, but eating from God's tree, the all-knowing tree (or what I like to refer to it as the "Know-It-All Tree"), they can begin functioning *like* Him. When I think about what being God means, I have to refer back to His attribute of being all-knowing, because when you are all-knowing, you are the supreme judge, you know what's right and wrong, what's good and evil, because you can see into the heart of man and you know everything.

So, the serpent planted two lies in the heart of man that have been passed down through the generations. They are: (1) God lies, so you can't trust Him and (2) you can be your own god and sit in judgment. For mankind, nothing has changed since that day; the Evil One still operates the same way and man still believes he can be God, judging right from wrong and controlling his or her little universe.

As we continue in Genesis chapter three, we see that both Adam and Eve took the bait and ate from the Know-It-All Tree, and what God said would happen in that day, (and might I say, in that moment) happened. They died. We know it wasn't a physical death, because Scripture indicates that Adam lived to be nine hundred years old (oy vey) and had many children. Death for them was a spiritual death, and spiritual death was the loss of everything they needed to live a fully functional spirit-life, a life lived in tandem with their Creator, heart to heart. In this moment, the man and woman lost their home, their belonging. They began to experience the brutal effects of spiritual death, which were accompanied by some pretty uncomfortable feelings like fear, shame, and guilt. Suddenly, their emotions became the determining factor that told them whether they were okay or not, as they began to depend on them to reveal truth.

"Then the eyes of both of them were opened, and they knew that they were naked; and they sewed fig leaves together and made themselves loin coverings." (Genesis 3:7)

Hadn't they always been naked? Yes. God created them naked and after creating them, He said it was good. Hadn't they always known they were naked? No, they did not, because they hadn't eaten from the Know-It-All Tree. And what came next is even more startling. They began to function *like* gods knowing right and wrong, good and evil. They saw that they were naked, and they made a judgment about it and decided that it was evil. Right out of the gate, they saw that they were not equipped to eat from this tree or to be *like* God.

When God confronted them, with their ridiculous fig

leaf get-ups, they began to do what man has done ever since: react. They reacted to the feelings produced from their spiritual death and began developing coping strategies like hiding, covering-up, and blaming.

Man sinned. What was the first sin committed in the Scriptures? It wasn't lying, cheating, adultery (although, they cheated on God, so to speak), or murder; it was very simple and it's the root of all sin: they chose independence from God. They chose to live independently, doing their own thing in their own way and, in essence, becoming their own god; setting it up for mankind to live a life apart from God doing what they wanted and judging everything and everyone else at the same time.

But God . . . His heart is always for us and the very first demonstration of grace came on the heels of the very first sin. "The Lord God made garments of skin for Adam and his wife, and clothed them" (Genesis 3:21). Where did God get garments of skin do you suppose? He didn't just pop into the nearest Bloomingdale's. He took an animal and He sacrificed it, skinned it, and covered them. God taught Adam and Eve that you must sacrifice an animal; the blood shed would cover their sins and they would have to do this perpetually every year at the appointed times. Adam and Eve taught their children to do the same, and so it went all through the Old Testament. The entire Book of Leviticus instructs about the sacrificial system.

When Adam and Eve began having offspring, the children brought their own sacrifices to God; Abel brought the first-born of his flock, which was acceptable to God, but Cain brought the fruits and vegetables from his harvest and he was chastised for it. Cain's coping mechanisms were not very positive. He was jealous of his brother and murdered him.

God's requirement of a blood sacrifice to cover Adam and Eve's sin was symbolic of a greater sacrifice that would not just cover sin, but completely remove it once and for all. The Hebrew word for *atone* means *kipporah*, which means to cover. This word is not used in the new covenant, since it is only an old covenant concept. In the Scriptures, the word *atonement* is not used to describe Jesus's death on the cross. Instead, Jesus' sacrifice and His blood completely eradicated sin—*all* sin—for those who believe, not merely covered it. "By this will we have been sanctified through the offering of the body of Jesus Christ *once for all*" (Hebrews 10:10, emphasis added).

God's second demonstration of grace was when Adam and Eve were driven from The Garden. "Then the Lord God said, 'Behold, the man has become like one of Us, knowing good and evil; and now, he might stretch out his hand, and take also from the tree of life, and eat, and live forever" (Genesis 3:22). Rather than live in a fallen state for all eternity, man was prevented from eating from the Tree of Life and thus became mortal and eventually died physically. Both the man and the woman, as well as their descendants, would have the opportunity for redemption through Messiah one day and be fully restored; once again, their hearts finding home.

Something else that Adam lost which is rarely noted is that while Adam was created in the image of God, his offspring were not. Only those who have been crucified with Messiah, died, and been resurrected to a new life are created anew with God's image and likeness. Genesis 5:1-3 says, "This is the book of generations of Adam. In the day when God created man, He made him in the likeness of God. He created them male and female, and He blessed them and named them Man in the day when they were created. When Adam had lived one hundred and thirty years, he become the father of a son *in his own likeness, according to his image,* and named him Seth." What does it mean to have God's likeness and image? The Scriptures don't really say, but it might mean that we share the same nature and identity, which Adam surely lost when he ate from the forbidden tree.

When God created man, He created him to need Him, to need life from Him and everything that pertains to life. He purposed that man should know who he was, to know his own identity. Life in God is where we find our identity. When you think about the things that pertain to life—the things that we need on a spiritual level that we experience on an emotional level—what probably comes to mind is everything that God is, His nature and character. The Fruit of the Spirit (love, joy, peace, patience, kindness, goodness, faithfulness, gentleness, and self-control), as well as forgiveness, wisdom, security, significance, and adequacy, are all things that are found in God; things that we need and, apart from God, don't have. As our needs are unmet, we live a dysfunctional existence in constant search for home, as I've stated previously, "a place" where we belong, where the light of the fire of God burns bright. Therefore, home is not only where the heart is but where the heart is made to live and flourish.

Growing up, my home was not the place where I felt I belonged. You always know that your kids are at home in their own house, if they bring their friends there. I wanted to be anywhere but there and my friends didn't much like coming to my home either. Irenie (my affectionate nickname for Mom) was anything but welcoming. She just didn't know how to relate to children, beginning with her own, but then neither did her own parents. As a result, I began a quest to find my home, to find God, that place where I belonged.

People need to know three basic things: that they are loved, that they are significant, and that they are secure. The degree to which they consistently experience these three things in their formative years will determine what they come to believe about themselves subconsciously; and, thus, set the course for how they live their lives. Even the most loving and nurturing parents fall short of providing what only God can give. Consequently, man's heart is constantly longing for home.

Movies and TV shows were continuous reminders that my heart longed for home. As a small child, one of my favorite shows was *Lassie*. If you were born in the 1950s, you must have loved *Lassie*. I can hear it now, the music at the introduction when the credits are rolling, "Lassie, come home!" as little Timmy calls for his beloved dog and my heart leaps at the sound. And in the movie the *Wizard of Oz* when Dorothy clicks those ruby red slippers and says, "There's no place like home, there's no place like home," again my heart stirs. A more contemporary movie that Ben and I watched together repeatedly when he was young was *Fly Away Home*, a story about a father and daughter who train a flock of abandoned geese to follow their ultra-light planes from Canada to a winter home in North Carolina. Last of all, my mom used to love Christmas carols, the secular ones, the ones I call holiday music. Her favorite one was *I'll Be Home for Christmas*, because Christmas Eve was her birthday and it reminded her of her family back in Baltimore. She too longed for home; a memory of a time long ago, never to be found again. So, you see, our search for *home* represents a longing to be somewhere we belong, where we are most loved and most content; where we were meant to be.

In light of what I've shared, it doesn't take much education or brainpower to see that since the fall of man, people have searched near and far to find their heart's content in everything but God, whether it be in wealth, career, relationships, sex, children, marriage, recognition, achievement, body image and eternal youth, or religion. There are endless ways that a person can try to meet their needs for love, significance, and security; and I have exhausted most of them myself. However, there are a couple of problems with self-sufficient living, aside from the fact that it doesn't work. First, we are created for God alone to meet our needs, so naturally it's not going to work. Second, God is the Source of everything we need whether it's love, significance, or security. Therefore, anything we experience outside of the Source is counterfeit at best. What we can experience in God is the real thing because He *is* love, He *is* significance, and He *is* security. However, what we settle for apart from Him is a momentary sensation or an imitation. That which is momentary is based solely on a feeling that's fleeting and that's totally dependent upon our efforts to keep that feeling going. For example, if I am dependent on my relationships to know that I am loved, significant, and secure; then I feel those things when the people with whom I'm in relationship (spouses, children, friends, and associates) are meeting my expectations. But what happens if my child steals money from me? What do you think I might feel? I can tell you, because it happened back in the day, repeatedly, and I felt unloved, insignificant and insecure, as well as a few other things. Being dependent on anyone or anything other than God to meet our needs will lead us to have to control our circumstances and control how people behave. However, if I am dependent on God as my source for love, significance, and security, my source is not going to change even when circumstances and people in my life aren't ideal. That's not to say I'm not going to feel things, but if I know where my home is and I'm depending on the eternal, as opposed to the temporal, The Source instead of a resource; my heart and my belonging will remain at home and intact.

Here are some important truths about God that should impact how we relate to Him:

- And my God will supply all your needs according to His riches in glory in Christ Jesus. (Philippians 4:19)
- God is Light, and in Him there is no darkness at all. (1 John 1:5)
- I am The Way, The Truth and The Life. (John 14:6a)
- God is love, and the one who abides in love abides in God, and God abides in him. (1 John 4:16b)
- God has given us eternal life, and this life is in His Son. He who has the Son has the life; he who does not have the Son of God does not have the life. (1 John 5:11-12)
- Gracious is the Lord, and righteous; Yes, our God is compassionate. (Psalm 116:5)

Based on what His Word says, God meets all of our needs, He is the Light and the source of all truth, He is compassionate and gracious, He is love and He is the Life—eternal life—the life that we need in order to be full and complete. Our feelings will never truthfully answer the questions we have about our identity—am I loved, am I significant, and am I secure? Unfortunately, most people rely on their feelings to answer those questions, which leads them to living life trying to control circumstances and people in an effort to feel okay; and if they feel *okay*, they believe they are *okay*, which isn't *okay*!

I lived this way for most of my life, but when I discovered these truths and began looking to Jesus as my Source, things began to change for me. I used to depend on boyfriends, girlfriends, and later my husband and kids to fill my emotional tank, so to speak. Sometimes it felt like they were meeting my emotional needs and other times, I was left feeling empty. At that point, I would try to get them to step it up and fly right, so I would feel better. God can certainly use your spouse, child, or a friend as a resource, but it becomes a problem when we are dependent on the resource instead of God as the Source.

Finding our hearts at home in Jesus is coming to the realization that He is so much more than The Savior who took away our sins and paid off our debt, He is our life; the new life that we have been placed into. There is this intimacy that we can experience in our relationship with Him that was absent prior to the Cross. Ever since the Garden, He has been calling our hearts home that we might know Him in an intimate way, as He truly is and not as we've been conditioned by life to believe He is.

There are days that are so demanding and exhausting that I just can't take one more thing going wrong, one more problem, or one more challenge to face. We all have those days and when we do, God reminds us that He is still God and He is sovereign above all else. It's the challenges and pain we experience in life that expose our need for God. We cannot live a spiritually functional life apart from Him.

It could be the death of a loved one, a terminal diagnosis, a marriage falling apart, or a million other reminders that this is not our home. These are the times when we need the wild, unrestricted love of God to remind us that it's going to be okay, even when life is not okay. *We're* going to be okay. When we turn to Him, His steady assurance of His tenderness and compassion is there for us. What we need from God are His strong arms wrapped around us, and a gentle whisper that quiets our anxious soul, and satisfies our deepest, heartfelt longing. That's home.

Everywhere around us are reminders that God IS and His love for us will never fail; however, we keep forgetting the most important thing: remember God! Remember who He is. He is faithful and He created us in order to love us and to be in intimate union with us. He wants to be our "go to" for everything. When we encounter troubles, is running to Jesus our immediate response or do we run to our resources, like our spouse or a friend? When we choose to deal with problems apart from God, we can't help but create greater problems and pain for ourselves as we rely on false gods; seeking life from empty cisterns and trying desperately to find what our hearts really need.

The Lord said to the Israelites after delivering them from slavery in Egypt, "*Remember* that you were slaves . . . and that the LORD your God brought you out of there with a mighty hand and an outstretched arm" (Deuteronomy 5:15, emphasis added). Remember! We need reminders because we continuously forget who God is and all the things he has done for us in the past. Our present troubles are simply more opportunities for us to remember that God is for us, that Jesus is enough, and that when we call on Him, He is ready and waiting to act on our behalf. Mountains are going to fall, giants will be overthrown, and walls will come tumbling down with a mighty shout of faith when we give our burdens to Jesus.

A heart that is lost and floundering, looking for that someone or something to cling to is a heart that is lonely and broken. There isn't enough money to fix it, enough plastic surgery to prop it up, enough friends, family, or lovers to fill it. Only Jesus can give what the heart needs.

But there's just one last thing about God that makes life in Him less appealing than all the other resources, like Buddha, Krishna, and the New Age movement, being peddled in the world today. Brennan Manning said it best in his book *Signature of Jesus*, "We will find ourselves not on the path to power but on the path to powerlessness; not on the road to success but on the road to servanthood; not on the broad road of praise and popularity but on the narrow road of ridicule and rejection. To be like Christ somehow we must lose our life in order to find it. Christianity preaches not only a crucified God, but also *crucified men and women.*" This is not a popular, crowd-pleasing message. The *New York Times* best-seller's list is not brimming with books on this topic. "Hey, come accept Jesus as your life, so you can spend half of it, or more, in the valley and give up all the rights to what you think you deserve!"

Life in Jesus is a clarion call to death: death to your independence, death to your self-centeredness, and death to all those things you love and depend on more than God (your idols) to make you feel okay. When it comes to sitting on a throne, there's only room for One Person!

9

FINDING YOURSELF

Knowing yourself is the beginning of all wisdom.

—Aristotle

*N*ow that we've nailed down the truth *about* God, we've only unearthed half of the problem with living the Christian Life—as God Himself intended. Life is *in* Him, but if we don't know what *He* is really like, then we can't know who *we* are, since we are created in His image through a rebirth in Christ.

People are hardwired to see things either through a positive lens or a negative one. This is true even though we *can choose* to see things either way based on what we believe. To see everything through a positive lens is not necessarily better, since being positive can just be the way a person copes with difficulty and challenges, instead of trusting Jesus with the reality of one's situation. Conversely, being negative can work the same way. How do I know this? Well, what would you say if I told you that, for many years, Rachel's nickname for me has been Eeyore? That might tell you something about my hardwiring. In case you don't know Eeyore, he is the donkey in *Winnie the Pooh* who is generally characterized as pessimistic, gloomy, depressed, even anhedonic. He lacks pleasure and sees the dark cloud in everything. Although we laugh when she calls me Eeyore, there is some truth to it. So, there are Pollyannas in the world and Eeyores and I'm definitely no Pollyanna! I came from negative people. Not only was I wired that way, my environment was that way. Having said that, this inclination is not based on truth, because the truth is what God reveals to us in our valleys and sometimes the negative experience is actually a positive one and vice versa.

It's pretty challenging to find the positive in a fallen world where there is so much suffering and loss, where children are abused, and families are torn apart by war and people are dying horrific deaths from famine and disease. I weep inside when I see, in our own country, the effects of broken homes with children being raised by absentee single parents scratching out a living, homelessness, and violence (plus the desensitization toward it). Not to mention when all of this is combined with the absence of any real faith in God. How do you put a positive spin on that? Come on all you Pollyannas!

As a young child, I came face-to-face with the reality of death when my cat Boots died. I had him for seven years, which is not very long, unless you haven't been on the planet much longer than that. Boots meant everything to me growing up in a family where we didn't connect on a heart level. I felt alone as a child since Gordon and Rhoda were nine and thirteen years older than I. As for friends in my neighborhood my mother was pretty strict about my staying away from the *goyim*, as I mentioned earlier, so friends were in short supply. When Boots had gone missing, my mom soon found him, dead in the ivy in our backyard. She put him in a box and made my brother take him away. I was inconsolable, but my Mom's way of dealing with anything remotely emotional was to ignore it. So no one helped me through this loss, which left me with feelings of abandonment that followed me into my adult life. By the time Boots died, Rhoda, dealing with her own hurts and struggles, had moved out of the house. This was a significant loss since she had become like a surrogate mother for me. I remember being attached to her in a way I never was to our mom in those early years. No one explained Rhoda's absence to me, at least that I can recall. All I knew was that suddenly she was no longer in my life. Thus, my enormous feelings of abandonment had set the stage for future losses, starting with the loss of Boots.

Over my lifetime, each loss, great and small, has carried its own dimension of pain. I always say that the greater the love, the greater the loss, and the greater the pain. Some of those losses were the result of death and others, the unfortunate end of a relationship for reasons that have failed me at times.

As a young child, you don't sit and ponder life and what it's all about; you just live in the moment. For the average child growing up in the free world with all its modern comforts and conveniences, life just happens; if you're lucky, you look forward to carefree days of fun, school, and family time. Life is simple. But as we grow, experience teaches us that life is not as simple as we thought. It has its wonderful, exciting times and things to anticipate with great joy, but it's also filled with not-so-wonderful things; things that hurt us. We learn that we can't control what happens to us. We learn that we must take the good with the bad and allow it to make us want to give more, love more, and forgive more. The best thing we can possibly do in life is choose to be surrendered to God in it.

One of my favorite movies is *Soul Surfer*, the true story of a teen named Bethany Hamilton, who grew up in Hawaii. She began surfing as a little girl and dreamed of becoming a professional surfer one day. And then life happened. While out surfing with friends one day, she was brutally attacked by a shark and lost her arm. Bethany thought her life was over, and with it her dream of becoming a professional surfer. *But God . . .* He opened her eyes and revealed some truths to her about surfing and about life that changed Bethany forever.

In 1 Corinthians 13:11, Paul wrote, "When I was a child, I used to speak like a child, think like a child; when I became a man, I did away with childish things." The context of this verse is Paul's discourse about *love. Love* is what life is all about. This is what God revealed to Bethany through her tragic loss, a loss that God used for her good:

When you get caught in the impact zone, you need to get right back up. Because you never know what's over the next wave. And if you have faith, anything is possible, anything at all. (Bethany Hamilton, *Soul Surfer* (New York: Gallery Books, 2004)

The Bethany Hamiltons of the world were a great inspiration to me when Ken died. The magnitude of the pain came at me like a thirty-foot wave that left me completely undone; I couldn't breathe, it was so overwhelming. The psalmist wrote, "Even though I walk through the valley of the shadow of death, I will fear no evil, for you are with me" (Psalm 23:4). I was blindsided by death and by a valley

I was not prepared to face, but I knew that Jesus was with me.

WHO AM I?

Picking up the thread of *belonging* from the previous chapter, I'd like to illustrate a slightly different aspect of belonging, this time as it relates to identity. When I lost Ken, I began living a new reality. To my way of thinking, I no longer *belonged TO* anyone. When I was a child, I *belonged TO* Irene and Mickey Cohen. Then I *belonged TO* Ken (as much as he to me). I found myself in an identity crisis in this unfamiliar territory; feeling lost, alone, and quite frankly, terrified. *I don't belong to anyone, I'm unattached*, the loop kept playing in my head. That, I discovered, has been the lie the Evil One has been whispering in my ear since the day my sister left home.

I am with you, the Lord's quiet and assuring voice spoke to me. *You belong to me, Yolanda, you always have.* The truth is, I belonged to Him since I was in my mother's womb. What I knew in my intellect, I was now discovering on a whole new level that's making all the difference to me. I am experiencing Him "through the valley of the shadow of death." I'm experiencing my *home* and my identity in my Messiah. He is *with* me. Not only that, He is *in* me and I am *in Him* for all eternity. I am *attached TO* God. No one and nothing can change that reality.

I knew these biblical truths intellectually for a long time. I even taught them to countless men and women, but it's through my loss and time of grieving in this particular valley that I have come to truly know in my heart what I once knew only in my head. That's not to say that I don't miss Ken, but I'm not about to run out and find a husband just to have that again. God is teaching me each day, and each moment of each day, how to live life belonging only to Him; needing only Him and finding my identity only in Him. Even if He should call me to married life again, these truths will be firmly rooted in my heart. I thought they were firmly planted throughout my life with Ken, but when he died, God busted me! His death exposed deep wounds that I didn't even know were there and now God is in the process of healing me from them.

This journey of finding myself hasn't been easy, but I am keenly aware of the Lord's presence like never before. His grace continues to give me the strength to want to go on, to make a new life, to kick Eeyore in the ass (excuse the pun) and to trust Him in this valley and my future valleys.

Knowing who we are as children of God—finding our identity in Him—is one of the single most important pursuits in experiencing life in Jesus. Your identity is not in your marital status, nor your children, nor your reputation. It's not in your education, your career, or your popularity. It's not in your political affiliation, your financial status, or your performance, good or bad. You are not a good person because you do good things, nor are you a bad person because you do bad things. And you are not what you feel. Your identity comes from *to whom* you belong. You have been born into God's family and you now have His spiritual DNA. Everything about you that matters is based on who *He* is and what *He* says about you.

A believer who knows this has no need to strive to become someone, because they have already become who God has created them to be. They are complete in Messiah Jesus, lacking nothing. Therefore, they can rest, abide, and enjoy their life in Him. When a person knows their identity and knows that their Father in Heaven is good, no matter what life throws their way, they become truly free and not at the mercy of their flesh, the flesh of others, or any need to control their circumstances.

A believer who doesn't know who they are in Him, but assumes they still have their old identity—the identity into which they were first born (that is, Adam)—is going to live that way. If you believe that you are a rotten, undeserving, miserable sinner who must continually prove your worthiness as a child of God, just guess how you're going to live. You'll remain in a state of constant striving to be better; buying every self-help book that comes out and condemning yourself every time you sin; then begging God to forgive you and overlook your wretched flaws. You'll read Scripture about your identity in Messiah, about being forgiven, and about being an overcomer; but you won't believe it and because you won't believe it, you won't live it. The sad thing is that not only will you be miserable living that life, you will unwittingly bring glory to the Evil One who will be whispering to you, *I told you so, You're not one of them, You're a loser,* or *What kind of Christian do you think you are?*

A child of God who knows who he is brings glory to God by living dependently on Jesus. When he sins, he thanks God that his sins are already forgiven and that he's freed from the law of sin and death. He walks in truth, holding his head high, choosing truth over lies, and choosing Jesus over feelings. He rests in His finished work on the cross, rather than his own achievements, his good performance, or his religious activity. A child of God who knows their identity walks in faith and never gives up. They hope in all things and accept that they are on a journey of growth to know Jesus more; not on a path of striving to become a better Christian. Their identity is firmly rooted in their spiritual birth and in the likeness of Jesus, and not in their behavior.

CATERPILLARS AND BUTTERFLIES

The process of metamorphosis is the best analogy to illustrate what happens when someone who is "in Adam" dies and is reborn into a new life, "in Jesus." When we are made new, our spirit is regenerated, and we become a brand new creation. Most Christians fundamentally think of themselves as the same old person, but with a new veneer. Every time I hear a believer say, "I'm just a sinner saved by grace," I want to shake them, "NO! Haven't you read your Bible? That's not what God says!" The fact is that as a believer, you're a saint; a redeemed, holy, and righteous one that sometimes sins; but "sinning" is not your identity any more than praying and going to church make you a Christian. Behavior does not determine identity for a child of God; spiritual birth does. So when the caterpillar becomes a butterfly, he's no longer a caterpillar. He's not even a caterpillar with wings; he's a completely new species.

> Therefore, if anyone is in Christ, he is a new creation.
> The old has passed away; behold, the new has
> come. (2 Corinthians 5:17, ESV)

When I was a new believer, I still felt a lot of remorse, guilt, and shame about my life prior to my salvation experience. I did things and was involved in things that, as a child of God, continued to haunt me. I knew I was forgiven, but I just couldn't get past the shame. I had only been a believer for a few years when the Lord showed me the Corinthians verse. It became my life verse. From that moment on, I knew I was not the old Yolanda. She died and was buried with Christ and the person who emerged with Christ from the grave was new.

> No one puts new wine into old wineskins; otherwise the wine will burst the skins, and the wine is lost and the skins as well; but one puts new wine into fresh wineskins."
> (Mark 2:22)

> Or do you not know that all of us who have been baptized [placed] into Christ Jesus have been baptized [placed] into His death? Therefore we have been buried with Him through baptism into death, so that as Christ was raised from the dead through the glory of the Father, so we too might walk in newness of life. For if we have become united with Him in the likeness of His death, certainly we shall also be in the likeness of His resurrection, knowing this, that our old self was crucified with Him, in order that our body of sin might be done away with, so that we would no longer be slaves to sin; for he who has died is freed from sin.
> (Romans 6:3-7)
> (Note that *sin* throughout this passage is used as a noun, not a verb.)

> Moreover, I will give you a new heart and put a new
> spirit within you; and I will remove the heart of
> stone from your flesh and give you a heart of
> flesh. I will put My Spirit within you and cause
> you to walk in My statutes, and you will be
> careful to observe My ordinances.
> (Ezekiel 36:26-27)

As a brand new creation, we have a new heart and a new spirit; plus, we have God's Spirit living in us. Everything about us is new, with the exception of two things: we don't *feel* new and we don't *think* new. These are aspects of ourselves that change based on how God works to renew our minds and transform how we live; in short, as we grow in the grace of God. No quick process either, I might add! It takes a lifetime of walking with Him and experiencing His Life in us.

When devastating things happen to people, there can be a tendency to make that horrible event their identity. It becomes their banner; what they believe defines them as a person. Our experiences (good and bad) may shape us, but they don't define us. We can be truly defined by nothing except who we are as a result of our birth, either in Adam or in Jesus. We are not defined by the opinions of others; or the grade we got on an algebra test.

YOUR FATHER'S NATURE

I mentioned that I am a lot like my earthly dad. It's because I have his DNA, not because he raised me, or I lived in the same house with him. It's because I was born from him (in Adam) and got his traits. Well, the same is true for a Christian, even if that Christian still thinks and acts like a caterpillar. We possess the same DNA: the same traits, the same desires, the same nature and heart. When we come to know we have the nature and heart of God, we will begin to act like it. The Deceiver wants us to believe that we still have the old nature and a desperately wicked heart and will use our performance to prove it, but it's all based on false beliefs and teachings that are not rooted in Scriptures.

So while I am a new creation, I live in a fallen world where people get sick and die, where tragedies happen and where we experience pain and loss of all kinds. God's kids are not exempt from these things. I can't imagine what my life would be like without all the valleys. They have shaped me and grown me into the person I am today and will be tomorrow, in terms of trusting God and allowing Jesus to live in and through me.

I'm still grieving and growing through this valley. God only knows what's around the corner. Like Scarlet, I'll think about that tomorrow! But I've learned that I can't control my grief or my growth, Only God does. And time.

DON'T ASK WHY

To love another person is to see the face of God.

—Victor Hugo, *Les Misérables*

here's no denying that everywhere we look in this world there's pain and suffering. We don't have to go to Africa or India to find it; we have plenty of it here in the USA. The six o'clock news is a constant reminder. Often the reaction to pain and suffering, even that of another's, is a pointed finger at God. "God is the reason we suffer," we say, "because He can alleviate it, but doesn't." Again, God is the Cosmic Meanie looking down on humanity and dispensing all sorts of pain and suffering upon mankind. Maybe you're in the Cosmic Meanie camp or maybe you're in the camp that dares to suggest that pain and suffering does *not* come from God, but from man's own choice to live independently from God or from the schemes of the Evil One; both of which started in the Garden of Eden. I camp in the latter group.

Throughout Scripture, in both the Old Testament and the New Testament, we see the evidence of God's redeeming work, *through* the pain and suffering inherent in a broken and fallen world. In the previous chapter, I alluded to the idea that what we call *good*, God often calls *evil*, and what we call *evil*, God often calls *good*. The bottom line is that God is the best one to make that judgment, not us. Since the beginning of time, God knew every evil thing that would happen and He already had a plan in place to redeem, restore, and renew. God takes the mess we make with the Evil One's help and turns it around, making something spectacular out of it.

While in the midst of the pain and suffering, it's a normal human reaction to want to know why, since the *why* is often hidden from us. Why should so many people lose their homes in a wildfire that sweeps across thousands of acres of dry mountainsides, or in a flood caused by unusual rainfall and ill-equipped dams, or in a freak tsunami? Why should so many lose their lives or the lives of their loved ones at the hands of vicious terrorists? Why should mothers I've counseled have to bury their children due to auto accidents and illnesses? Why them and not me? And somehow we believe that knowing why will make the loss or the devastation easier, but that's not true. In fact, knowing that the reason your child died in an auto accident was because the other driver was drunk or not paying attention certainly does not diminish your pain. In fact, it may even intensify it to know that it could have been prevented.

I spent years of my walk with Jesus asking God why. Perhaps the answer was obvious: to learn to just trust Him, but I kept asking. Once our promised baby boy finally came along, I agonized daily as I watched him struggle in his life and I asked why. *I give you what you need and not what you want,* was all I heard, the same answer He gave me to Rachel's question in Hawaii so long ago. When Ben started down a path that led to a criminal life, drugs, incarceration, and ultimately a child born outside of marriage; I asked why. *I'm going to redeem his life,* came the answer.

The truth is, *why* is the wrong question. The more important question is *why not.* I don't know why things happened in my life or in my family's, but why shouldn't such suffering and loss happen to us? My son could have easily overdosed and died. I spent years anticipating having to bury him, but instead I buried my husband. There was nothing that could have prevented a brain tumor; it was just the roll of the dice. Why shouldn't we suffer losses living in a broken and evil world? Why should anyone expect to sail through this life unsinged by death or tragedy, and the resulting pain that knocks the wind out of you? Have we bought into some fairytale that life should be nothing but rainbows and unicorns?

I don't ask why anymore, because it doesn't matter. The only thing that matters is what the heck we do when our world is rocked. For those who don't know God, it can define them. It defined me before I became a believer. I was desperate for Him and I didn't even have the kind of suffering in my life then that I would have later as a believer in Jesus. For those of us who know Him, who have walked with Him, and understand the crucified life, He is the only answer to our question. Jesus must be our sanctuary in the midst of our pain, our shelter in the storm, our security and rock when the ground under our feet is crumbling. He is our light in the darkness leading us, our wisdom when nothing makes any sense, and our hope when we are at the end of ourselves and in utter despair.

Sometimes I just have to turn off all the news media, because I can't take any more horror or evil. It's not that I want to put my head in the sand and pretend it's not happening, because I know all too well that it is. It's the magnitude of the pain and hurt in this world, the negativity and hopelessness disseminated by the media that make money off of misery. It can be overwhelming, particularly so when you realize there isn't much you can do about it, except try to impact your own sphere of influence.

IT'S ABOUT LOVE

There are a million and one ways to define life depending on one's history, theology, age, socio-economic standing, and perhaps one's current circumstances. Life is pretty simple, regardless of the vantage point from which we define it—just embarking on life or nearing its end, rich or poor, ecstatic or in the depths of despair. It's about love. The Beatles wrote the song, "All You Need Is Love" and they were right. I believe that is why God created us—to love and be loved—and the source of that love is in God Himself (1 John 4:7-8). However, what was intended to be pretty simple and straightforward quickly became something quite different. Love was no longer our purpose in life, because of what happened in the Garden. Instead, life became a matter of survival-of-the-fittest, getting mine, and taking care of me. It became about protecting ourselves from possible pain and, of course, trying to stay in control; the idea being that if we can stay in control, it keeps others from controlling us. This is, in fact, man's basic and most insidious problem and has been since the Garden.

Growing up with a controlling mother, I became resistant to controllers. The same was true of my siblings; we all like to be in control. We all think we have the answers. We all gravitate toward people who aren't *overt* controllers, people who control *covertly*, through people-pleasing and submission. Having an overtly controlling parent and two overtly controlling older siblings who told me what to do, when to do it, and how to do it, became, perhaps, a perfect trifecta! So, it was not rocket science that I would find happiness married to a man that was a covert controller. He was dominant in his work life and socially, but at home, Ken was much more comfortable allowing me to make decisions and then being willing to take the blame for them if they didn't work out. He did not like conflict, and he wanted everyone to like him. I, on the other hand, did not roll that way. When the kids were growing up, I became the "bad guy" and he was the support staff, just going with the flow, which was his covert method of staying in control. He and I eventually discovered that it only works for so long and then delivery day comes and you have to pay the piper for your ways of trying to meet your needs apart from God.

Many believers think that God gave us the Law to try to control us, but the opposite is true. He gave us the Law to expose our inability to obey it. Sounds kind of crazy, right? Well, I often say that God is a mystery and can appear to be obtuse! "'For my thoughts are not your thoughts, nor are your ways my ways,' declares the LORD. 'As the heavens are higher than the earth, so are my ways higher than your ways and my thoughts than your thoughts'" (Isaiah 55:8-9).

Somewhere along the way we lost sight of the main point, which is love. Love got lost in man's need to control and be comfortable and safe. When God gave us the Law, we placed our trust in it, looking to these laws as a way to make life work. Even when God gave life in Himself through Jesus Christ, we continued to try to find life in laws. Our ideas about love got lost in fairytales, romance novels, and Hallmark cards. We reduce love to *a feeling* instead of *action*, confusing sex and lust with love. Authentic love is a demonstration of giving one's self to another in a sacrificial way. When couples say they divorce because they fell out of love, what they really mean is that the passion, the feelings, and physical desire are no longer there.

A while ago, I made the mistake of making a New Year's resolution, which I usually didn't do, since they are an immediate set-up for failure. My resolution, my prayer really, was to learn to love more. Ya know, the moment those words came out of my mouth, I knew I was asking for it—kind of like praying for patience. Love is something we already have in abundance, because it is a part of who we are even though we might not always walk in it. So I knew a lesson was on its way.

The Evil One wants to instill fear and keep us from what is in our heart of hearts. And the desire of my heart, to love more, was the real me; God put that desire there. Of course, I had no idea how the Lord would bring about the answer in my life, but He wastes no time and certainly has plenty of specially-designed opportunities on hand for me and my crew.

It should have been no surprise that Benjamin became the primary player in this "love story" as I was recuperating from foot surgery. He had moved back home and had plans to return to college and get involved in some kind of church ministry. We were seeing some positive changes in him when we received the news that he was going to be a father. Rachel and her family just happened to be living with us at the time. Yeah, it was a real fun time.

After everything I'd been through with this child—two boarding school expulsions, two rehabs, and a year and a half of jail (and don't even ask me how many therapists we had been through; last time I counted, it was sixteen)—I was left in complete shock and despair. It was as if everything in my life went from color to black and white in one announcement. How I wished I was in a deep sleep and could awake from this nightmare, but this was no dream; this was real. I had nowhere to go with this, but God. It was a pretty short prayer, because I just didn't know what to pray, but I needed His wisdom and was desperate to hear from Him. I did have one question for God, and it was this: *Lord, why have you not answered my prayers for Ben?* There's the *why* question again. He didn't answer.

In the course of that week, I struggled with a myriad of feelings and a bucket load of anger, the contents of which I deposited in all the appropriate places and in the appropriate ways because I was flying by the instruments and could only do what I knew would bring resolution for me; namely, forgiving my son, cancelling all the emotional debts I believed he owed me, and surrendering all "my rights." Peace slowly flooded my soul once again. Black and white began to shift to color, color resuming its place in the picture that God was painting.

Then the Lord told me that He was, in fact, answering my prayer. Thank you, Lord. It's about time. It hit me right between the eyes: He was answering my New Year's prayer "to love more," and He did it in the most unexpected way, the way God always seems to show up.

Again, God never does things the way I would do them. I think I have pretty good ideas and plans, but He always trumps them. He's absolutely insistent on doing things His way and in His time to reach His desired goal, which is to redeem that which is lost and broken and bless our lives to bring glory to Him. That's God's MO and that's because He alone is God. Why do we even think we can do His job?

The night Ben broke the big news, I had been watching the movie version of the *Velveteen Rabbit* with my granddaughter, Maddie. Perhaps you're familiar with the story. It's about a young boy named Toby whose mother dies and his father sends him to live with his grandmother. Toby is lonely and feels abandoned by his father but fills his time and finds solace in his grandmother's attic playing with the toys up there. Here's an excerpt:

> *'What is REAL?' asked the Rabbit one day, when they were lying side by side near the nursery before Nana came to tidy the room. 'Does it mean having things that buzz inside you and a stick-out handle?'*
>
> *'Real isn't how you are made,' said the Skin Horse. 'It's a thing that happens to you. When a child loves you for a long, long time, not just to play with, but REALLY loves you, then you become Real.'*
>
> *'Does it hurt?' asked the Rabbit.*
>
> *'Sometimes,' said the Skin Horse, for he was always truthful. 'When you are Real you don't mind being hurt.'*

Just like in the story, when we give our heart to someone, it is going to hurt. We have two choices: avoid the hurt, which means avoid the love, or choose love and be willing to be hurt. I had been deeply hurt by Benjamin more times than I cared to count, and I often thought there would come a day that he would cross a line and that would be it; but the Lord has given me a new paradigm about love, *His* love. There's no line to cross with God. His love is eternal and is not dependent on the object, but the Giver. He loves whether we love back or not. He loves whether we behave or not. His love is constant, no matter what we do or say. If you want to love like He loves, we have to love Him more than all others and let Him love through us.

"When you are Real you don't mind being hurt." I'm not sure that I would agree with Skin Horse and say I don't mind, but I would say that love is worth hurting for if you're real. Being real is walking in your identity as a believer in Jesus, who you truly are at your core.

> *'Does it happen all at once, like being wound up,' he asked, 'or bit by bit?'*
>
> *'It doesn't happen all at once,' said the Skin Horse. 'You become. It takes a long time. That's why it doesn't happen often to people who break easily, or have sharp edges, or who have to be carefully kept. Generally, by the time you are Real, most of your hair has been loved off, and your eyes drop out and you get loose in the joints and very shabby. But these things don't matter at all, because once you are Real you can't be ugly, except to people who don't understand.'*
>
> *'I suppose you are real?' said the Rabbit. And then he wished he had not said it, for he thought the Skin Horse might be sensitive. But the Skin Horse only smiled.*
>
> *'The Boy's Uncle made me Real,' he said. 'That was a great many years ago; but once you are Real you can't become unreal again. It lasts for always.'*

As the story proceeds, Toby deeply loves the Rabbit, and because of his love, the Rabbit becomes Real. At the very end of the movie version, two of the toys in the attic realize that it's not *love* that makes you Real but *loving*!! It's about giving that love to another not just when they deserve it, but especially when they don't!

In that that moment, I heard the Father say to me, *Yolanda, it's all about loving. This is who you are and how I made you. This is the only reality you have. Loving your son, regardless of what he's done.* "Greater love has no one than this that one lay down his life for his friends" (John 15:13). Painful? Yes. Costly? Most definitely. This child that my son fathered is now seven years old. His name is Jacob and he is a wonderful gift from God. I don't ask *why* anymore, because it is plain to see that God used Jacob to give Ben the motivation and desire to be the kind of dad he had. I have watched my son step up to the plate and assume his responsibilities as a father, loving his son and teaching him just the way his dad did. He takes him to baseball games, skateboarding parks, fishing, Sunday school, and camp (the same camp Ben went to as a little boy). He works two jobs so he can afford to provide for him. Recently, he was awarded full custody of Jacob, since living with his mother was not a healthy or safe environment for him.

We may not always know the whys in life or understand God's ways, but we can know this: there isn't anything that happens to His children that He isn't going to redeem and use for good in some way. No matter how crazy or unreasonable, or outrageously and ridiculously tragic, He will always do something redemptive with it, if we let Him.

Asking God *why* negates my faith and trust in a Sovereign and Faithful God. Once again, it means I'm going back to the Know-It-All Tree trying to gain a sense of control and security by figuring things out and finding answers, when I really need to be content in believing that God has the answers and is working all things out for my good. Great minds and philosophers throughout history have all asked the same questions and most of those questions remain unanswered. Only God knows, because it's only *for* Him to know. We are designed to live dependently on Him, not independently. We are designed to walk in faith, not in feelings and having all the answers. We are meant to rest in His goodness. This has been the lesson of every valley in which I've walked. God is growing me to walk in love, forgiveness, and surrender by appropriating my identity in Him.

YOUR GET-OUT-OF-JAIL-FREE CARD

To forgive is to set a prisoner free and discover
the prisoner was you.

—Corrie Ten Boom

Christians often misunderstand what forgiveness really is or what it entails. A typical approach to forgiveness is going to the person who hurt you and telling them what they've done. Not only is this ineffectual, it doesn't, even remotely, come close to what forgiveness actually is or how to approach it. If someone said something hurtful to you, even unintentionally, and you go to them and tell them that what they said that hurt you, what do you think their knee-jerk reaction would be? They might become defensive and say they didn't mean to hurt you and begin to justify themselves or they might completely invalidate you by telling you that you shouldn't be hurt. Then you would spend thirty minutes or more talking with them and trying to reconcile. Most would call that "forgiveness."

When you have lots of hurts, you have lots of need to forgive. The deeper the hurt the more urgent it is. This was true in my relationship with my dad. When I was young, I just wanted my daddy's attention and to know that he loved me and was proud of me, but I never really got that message from him. Fathers are an important influence in a child's early development. Boys find their manhood and virility, or lack thereof, from their dads and girls discover everything there is to know about the opposite sex from them. Fathers shape a child's perspective not only about themselves and their acceptability in their masculinity or femininity, but also about their understanding and beliefs about God, the Supreme Father.

My dad was a passionate golfer and he played every Sunday, until he retired and then he played every day. One particular Sunday, my mom coaxed him into taking me to the driving range to teach me how to hit balls. I was so excited, mostly to get to do something with just me and my dad. I must have been nine or ten years old. He bought the bucket of balls and showed me how to stand properly and hold the club and swing. My enthusiasm didn't last long. Apparently, I was not doing it right, and he grew increasingly frustrated and started yelling at me. I came from a family of yellers. I rode home crying as he continued to yell. This became a theme in my life, *You never do anything right*. In retrospect, I see that my dad's own identity and sense of adequacy was attached to his children's performance and because I wasn't performing according to his expectation, it was, in his mind, a reflection on him. Remember, I said that I was a lot like my dad? Well, he grew up with the same theme in his life and I was his built-in confirmation!

When I was old enough to learn how to drive a car and get my license, my dad decided that he should be the one to teach me. I was ready for the challenge, but not without some caution by this time. We got in the car and drove to a quiet spot in the Valley, and he had me sit in the driver's seat. He proceeded to explain the brake, the accelerator, and the turn signal (thank God it was an automatic transmission). He then had me shift into drive and begin accelerating slowly. I'm thinking, *I can do this*. After all, I'd driven my friends' cars and several of those were standard shift, not that I mastered them. Instead of slowly moving forward, I lunged into full speed, unused to the car's nuances and, in panic, slammed on the brakes. After my dad's head jerked back, he screamed that I would never learn and took me home. Again, I was in a state of tears and defeat. *You will never learn* was added to the arsenal of lies I believed well into adult years.

After years of rejection from my father and the subsequent feelings of being unloved, unwanted and completely inadequate; a bitter resentment, even hatred, toward him began to take root inside of me; keeping me locked up in an emotional jail cell. All the things I began to believe about myself became my distorted "truth." It was from this "truth" that I lived. It became the motivation for me to prove to myself that it wasn't true by learning as much as I possibly could about things, so I could be right and do things right and feel good about myself.

As a child, no one tried to help me cultivate any interests or motivate me to pursue things that I might be talented in, except for my art. I loved to draw and paint and had a talent for it that came from my mother's side of the family. While she never really pursued anything artistic, she did have some talent and so did one of her sisters.

In my early twenties, I began to paint, and after a while, the paintings all had a biblical or Judaica theme. The more I painted, the better I became as an artist. I took some classes at the community college to improve my skills and, after a while, I was receiving a lot of attention within the faith community. I began selling my work and entering it in various art shows. My mom was proud of me. She loved my artwork and was a huge supporter of mine. My father, on the other hand, not so much. One time my parents were visiting us, and I was showing them my most recent work. My mom was impressed for several reasons. First of all, I had already been a believer in Jesus for many years and my life revolved around Him and anything to do with Him and all of my artwork reflected that. As I mentioned earlier, my mom was a docent at the Skirball Hebrew Cultural Center in LA, so she and I shared our interest in Jewish art. I always painted a Messianic Jewish theme. My dad didn't like it because it was "religious," and he was not religious. His response to my artwork was, "Can't you paint anything different, like landscapes or something?" Well, that was just an echo from my past, *You can't do anything right,* and I was hurt. Once again, there was nothing I could do to win my dad's approval.

Over and over again, the messages I received confirmed to me that I did not measure up in his eyes and naturally, in my mind, I projected that on to the eyes of God and everyone else in my life. I was never good enough or smart enough and the slightest hint of rejection made me work all the harder at winning people's approval.

I had stored up bucket loads of anger toward my father, and I really didn't know what to do with it. When I became a believer in Jesus, I forgave him in the only way I understood it at the time, but the feelings kept getting stirred up and the deeply ingrained lies kept surfacing, which only kept me in a perpetual state of hostility toward him. I tried very hard to temper it, but it typically came out through sarcastic remarks and poking fun at him, which he ignored. In retrospect, he probably felt rejected by me and withdrew even more, because rejected people reject people. Unbeknownst to me, all this anger, packaged as missed expectations (of love and acceptance from my earthly dad), imprisoned me. In spite of my feelings toward him, I was a dutiful daughter and cultivated a close relationship with my parents throughout my married years.

BREAKING THE CHAINS

About five years before my dad died at eighty-three, Gordon called me from LA to tell me that Mom had a heart attack and was in the hospital recovering, but someone needed to stay with Dad. Dutiful daughter that I was, I booked my flight to go out there and stay with him for a week. *Oh, no! I'm going to spend a whole week virtually alone with him! Oy.* All sorts of feelings bubbled to the surface, so I asked one of my colleagues (another staff counselor at Grace Ministries) to spend some extended prayer time with me. During that time of prayer, the Lord showed me exactly where the source of my pain began with my dad. Reliving the painful memories, the tears began to flow, and the Lord spoke straight into my heart. This was many years ago, but I've never forgotten His words, because they broke the chains that kept me in jail all those years. *Yolanda, I am your dad,* He said. Pretty simple, right? But when the Lord speaks to you, it's powerful. Never before had I referred to or even thought about God, the Creator of the Universe, as *Dad*. Immediately, the anger toward my earthly dad was gone and compassion took its place. Compassion for a man who never could win the approval of, or experience meaningful love from, his own parents. It flooded my soul. I wept for him and for myself, as it became apparent to me how the sins of the fathers were passed down through the generations.

Keeping mercy for thousands, forgiving iniquity and transgression and sin, and that will by no means clear the guilty; *visiting the iniquity of the fathers upon the children*, and upon the children's children, unto the third and to the fourth generation. (Exodus 34:7, KJV, emphasis added)

Well, you know what they say, "The proof of the pudding is in the tasting." I spent the entire week with my dad, taking him to the hospital to see Mom, going out to dinner, cooking his favorite meals and listening to him share the same stories I've heard, on repeat, my whole life. Something changed in our relationship, something subtle enough that an onlooker wouldn't even notice, but I could tell there was a difference. Dad was connecting with me and for the first time in my life, a healthy father-daughter attachment was forming.

SCALING THE WALL OF ANGER

Anger is a powerful and often destructive emotional reaction that, if left unresolved, can keep us locked up in a prison of our own making. Anger is a coping mechanism, a self-protective way to keep from feeling vulnerable and exposed. As long as a person stays angry, it will be hard to actually *feel* the feelings of being unloved, worthless, rejected, insignificant, insecure, or unwanted. These feelings lie beneath. In this sense, the anger becomes our way of protecting ourselves from the pain and vulnerability that follows.

In the case of my relationship with my dad, real forgiveness, which the Bible defines as "the cancelling of a debt" had taken place. I like to call it my "get-out-of-jail-free card," because I was the one, through my own unforgiveness and anger, who kept me locked up and it was true forgiveness that freed me.

> Be kind to one another, tender-hearted, forgiving
> each other, *just as God* in Christ also has forgiven
> you.
> (Ephesians 4:32, emphasis added)

> [Christ] having canceled out the certificate of debt
> consisting of decrees against us, which was
> hostile to us; and He has taken it out of the way,
> having nailed it to the cross.
> (Colossians 2:14)

> Bear with each other and forgive one another if any
> of you has a grievance against someone. Forgive
> as the Lord forgave you. (Colossians 3:13)

Notice that Paul says in Ephesians that we should forgive *just as God has forgiven us,* meaning, in *the same way* he has forgiven us. Well, how did God forgive us? Jesus went to the Cross and died, which cancelled the debt we owed God for our sin. Forgiveness is the cancellation of a debt, a significant event. The day I forgave my dad and cancelled the emotional debt I perceived he owed me, was a significant event for me; not one I will ever forget.

When someone is angry with you, you pretty much know it; they never really need to give it voice, because you feel their disapproval. I think my father felt my disapproval all those years. And, while he never admitted it until almost the end of his life, I think he knew he failed as a parent, especially with my brother and me. Now the anger was gone, and that emotional barrier was no longer keeping him from me, and he was able to experience my love and acceptance, which freed him to return it! You see, the power of forgiveness is an incredible gift that you can only give if you have received it first. So, I was able to pass to my earthly dad for the last five years of his life, the gift my Heavenly Dad first gave me; and in return, I was given the gift of love from him.

Prior to my life in Messiah, I would say that forgiveness did not come easily for me. If someone hurt me, I wanted to hurt them back by not forgiving them, which sounds ridiculous when you actually say it. What I didn't know is that not forgiving doesn't hurt my offender; it hurts me. The offender has long since moved on and forgotten all about what happened, or maybe doesn't even know that they said or did something to offend me.

What most people don't realize is that our expectations are directly linked to how we become offended. Imagine the amount of hurt that is eliminated or at least reduced when we don't put expectations on people. If my primary source for getting my need for love and acceptance met is God, then I'm probably going to be less offended when my loved ones behave unlovingly toward me. If there's someone in your life who makes you feel bad about yourself, it may very well be because you expect that person to fill your emotional tank for love and significance. As Christians, we are full and complete, our identity secured, and our needs already met in Him; which frees us to extend lots of grace when something innocent is said or done. Of course, there are times to confront and openly share about something when people get hurt in relationships, but most of the time we can let it go and recognize that we all do this at times; we all disappoint and fail to meet someone's expectations.

GOD'S FORGIVENESS

One of the biggest obstacles walking in forgiveness and cancelling someone's debt is one's feelings. How many times have you been deeply hurt by someone you love and actually *felt* like forgiving that person? Probably never. I've never *felt* like forgiving someone. When I think back to all the things that Ben did and how they hurt me, in no way did I *feel* like forgiving him. Based on my feelings, I wanted to line him up in front of a firing squad with an arsenal of verbal assaults! I also didn't passively wait until he came to me, sorry for what he did, either. Let me ask you this: when did God forgive us? Did He wait until we came to Him and said we were sorry? Of course not.

> And you were dead in your trespasses and sins, in
>   which you formerly walked according to the
>   course of this world, according to the prince of
>   the power of the air, of the spirit that is now
>   working in the sons of disobedience. Among
>   them we too all formerly lived in the lusts of our
>   flesh, indulging the desires of the flesh and of the
>   mind, and were by nature children of wrath, even

as the rest. But God, being rich in mercy, because of His great love with which He loved us, *even when we were dead in our transgressions*, made us alive together with Christ (by grace you have been saved), and raised us up with Him, and seated us with Him in the heavenly *places* in Christ Jesus, so that in the ages to come He might show the surpassing riches of His grace in kindness toward us in Christ Jesus.
(Ephesians 2:1-7, emphasis added)

For *while we were still helpless*, at the right time Christ died for the ungodly. For one will hardly die for a righteous man; though perhaps for the good man someone would dare even to die. But God demonstrates His own love toward us, in that *while we were yet sinners*, Christ died for us.
(Romans 5:7-8, emphasis added)

With Ben, I came to a point that every time he did something that hurt or offended me (yes, I had to continuously surrender my dependence on that peanut head to fill my emotional tank), I made a rational choice to forgive him by cancelling his debt. I chose to do this for no other reasons but the following: (1) It's my nature (in Christ) to forgive, (2) I'm not about to let someone else keep me in bondage, and (3) it's not about how I feel, but who I am. I forgive regardless of the offense and regardless of how many times that offense is repeated. Now that's not to say that anyone should continue in a trusting relationship with someone who is abusive. Perhaps, because of abuse and unhealthy patterns of behavior, relationships need to end or, at least, be tabled until the relationship can be a healthy and God-glorifying one.

Today when someone hurts me, I am quick to forgive. I do not hesitate to cancel that debt and move on, because if I don't, I'm just opening the door for the Evil One to make me miserable. Well, no thank you. Forgiveness is one thing I get to control.

IT IS FINISHED!

As a teenager and young adult developing my own ideas about life, my environment pretty much shaped my world-view. Growing up in LA and becoming a teenager in the late 1960s, with its anti-war protests, the drug culture and the music promoting those drugs, the sexual revolution, and my lack of any real moral compass coming from my home life; I was left without boundaries. I pretty much thought anything goes, as long as it doesn't hurt anyone else. Like a lot of kids my age, I was looking for belonging and an identity, which I found in the culture of the day. Needing desperately to be loved, since I never experienced that with my father, I lost my virginity at a young age and became sexually promiscuous, giving myself away physically and emotionally to anyone who would make me feel loved and wanted.

By the time I gave my heart to the Lord in the late 1970s, I had garnered a lot of regrets, but the thing I regretted the most was my abortion. After I gave my heart to Jesus and my life was His, I came to know I was forgiven. Not right away, however, because, sadly, I bought into a prevalent, though often unspoken, belief that your sins are forgiven *as you commit them, after asking for forgiveness for that sin*. In other words, on a sin-by-sin basis, triggering a sin-repent-sin cycle. To add to that, the Evil One uses our emotions to deceive us into believing that we aren't really forgiven at all. That lie kept me asking God to forgive me every week for every sin; at least for the ones I could recall. Perhaps, the once-and-for-all forgiveness that we have been offered just seems too easy, so we make it more difficult in order to ease our guilt and thus make it believable. *"It is finished!"* were Jesus' final words on the cross, as the Spirit left him (John 19:30). All of our sins were *future* sins at that point, ones we had not yet committed, because we were not yet born. Every sin we would ever commit was forgiven on the cross! In interpreting Scripture, people often do not consider context, audience, and syntax; and they do not compare and cross-reference passages. Perhaps the best example of this, as it relates to our so-called need to continually confess our sins, is 1 John 1:9, "If we confess our sins, He is faithful and righteous to forgive us our sins and to cleanse us from all unrighteousness." Typically, believers assume this means that (1) they must confess their sins every time they sin and (2) if they don't, they will not be forgiven. Very simply, if that is true, then forgiveness is no longer by grace, but is conditional. That interpretation does not stand-up against Romans 5, Hebrews 10, Ephesians 1 and 2, or Colossians 1:13-14, to name a few. Therefore, it must mean something else. When we look closely, we will discover that 1 John was a letter written to a mixed audience, addressing the current problem of the day, which was Gnosticism. The Gnostics believed that all matter is evil, and that knowledge is more important than faith, so they practiced esoteric mysticism. Of course, this belief is antithetical to what the disciples were teaching. The Gnostics didn't believe that you could sin, and John was addressing this heresy.

LETTING YOURSELF OFF THE HOOK

Receiving God's forgiveness for my abortion was one thing but forgiving myself was a whole other subject. Here's the problem with not forgiving yourself: it's like saying that you hold yourself to a higher standard than the God of the Universe does, which is bad enough, but then it says that what Jesus did on the cross was not enough. Whoa! When you frame it that way, which God did for me, forgiving yourself is not so difficult.

Since I made a mess of my life prior to my new life with Jesus, I believed I was a failure. Of course, the messages from my childhood validated that belief. When I became a believer in Messiah, I was determined to be a success. I had no idea, until years later, after I crashed and burned, that I was trying to earn my identity and become successful enough in my own eyes to forgive myself for my past. We live in a success-driven culture both in the Church and in the world. People strive to be successful in their careers, but also in their marriages, parenting, and friendships. Being successful is not a bad thing, but how people define "success" could very well lead them down the road of performing for the acceptance of others, and that's a road that leads to despair and frustration.

If we define success as most people do, by how well we're doing or by the end results, then we are living our life dependent on our own abilities and resources. Our faith is in "self-sufficiency" and we will fall into the trap of trying to control our circumstances and the people in our lives in order to fulfill our personal definition of becoming a successful parent, teacher, lawyer, friend, son or daughter, friend, or child of God.

How does God define our success? By two criteria:

Jesus's *performance* on our behalf and our faith. That's it! Jesus lived a perfect life. He never sinned. His perfect life fulfilled the righteous requirement of the Law, and then He gave *us* the credit for it. When we received His Life, we were given the gift of faith. When we place our confidence in what Jesus has done and appropriate it by faith, we can experience what's already true about ourselves—that we are successful!

Now if you want success by the world's standard, based on your own merit and get those pats on the back, recognition, and worldly applause; then you have to take the failure, despair, and disappointment that accompanies it. Basically, you are eating the fruit of the wrong tree, because only the Tree of Life can truly satisfy.

Unfortunately, God's definition of success and mine have not always lined up. What a surprise! I often find myself becoming critical of both myself and others. I never believed I was acceptable before I came to know the Lord. Then, once I knew Him and came to know intellectually that He accepted me, it didn't always translate into how I lived; because, deep down inside, I didn't truly believe I was acceptable. I have had to learn to accept myself, even when I'm at my worst, and even if others do not. The ability to love and accept ourselves just as God does is the root and foundation of our ability to love and accept others, especially God. If you can't tolerate what you see in others, then it is a sure bet that you are unable to tolerate the flaws you see in yourself; and that will hinder your ability to live and relate as one who is deeply loved and lovable.

To see yourself as God sees you—as you truly are—is to walk in the confidence of what happened at The Cross and to "put on the new self, which was created in righteousness and holiness" (Ephesians. 4:24). Don't buy into the Evil

One's schemes to get you to believe that because you don't always behave righteously or *feel* lovable and acceptable that you're not. You have two choices: (1) to believe what God's Word says about you or (2) to believe that who you and others are is based totally on the strength of performance. As I said, if you don't accept yourself, you can't accept others. Self-acceptance is pretty much an all-encompassing mind-set that says, in essence, "I am good enough and so are others." So when we are accepting, we project the love of the Father and agree with Him that we all have been made new, brand new. How does a person live and act like someone who believes he is perfectly lovable just the way he is? By treating others the same way, but you cannot do this through your flesh (on your own, apart from Christ). Only Jesus in you will live this way through you, without effort, as you rest in the truth of who you are in Him.

Back to my abortion, it was several years after becoming a believer before I could let myself off the hook for killing my unborn baby. I was already forgiven by God, but it seemed I could not escape my feelings of shame and guilt. The truth is that I was holding myself to a standard greater than God's. That is, until one day. Depending on your age, you may or may not remember singer and actor Pat Boone who found Jesus in his adult life and became an advocate for the unborn. I was home alone and flipping through the channels and landed, quite unplanned, on a Catholic network that I'd never seen before—and the singer caught my eye. I was curious to know what he was doing being interviewed by a nun. Well, the conversation was about a recent song he'd written for unborn aborted babies and his role as a voice for the pro-life movement. As I sat and took in the music, I could hear God's voice telling me that He had already forgiven me, but that it was time I forgave myself. There I was in the middle of my living room, crying, and letting go of the shame and guilt for what I had done and thanking God for His love and grace to bring me to that place of self-forgiveness. From that moment on, I never hesitated to speak publicly about my abortion or about the power of forgiveness, God's and my own.

THRIVING IN YOUR VALLEYS

During the years that I was trying to conceive and have a second child (technically, it would have been my third) I really battled with my anger at God and that intensified during all the years my son was "Livin' La Vida Loca," or "livin' the life" outside of God's plan for him. I didn't know what to do with that anger. It's pretty hard to trust God when you're angry with Him.

When Ken died, I expected that I would be angry with God. I was angry alright—angry at Ken's general practitioner who didn't run more extensive tests and angry with the medical team (except for his oncologist who gave it to me straight) for painting a rosy picture and making me believe there was hope. I was angry with life and the cards we'd been dealt, and I was angry when my best friend disappeared after giving my husband's eulogy at his memorial service. I had to do a lot of debt-cancelling and processing of all my feelings to get to the other side of that mountain of anger. Surprisingly, in the end, the one person with whom I was not angry was God. I think that score was settled with God when Benjamin was kicked out of PRC and sent back to jail. People often do direct their anger toward God, and I have done so in the past, as I shared earlier. I think all my past valleys, and finding God's grace and lovingkindness there, prepared me for this one. Plus, I don't believe that God gave Ken the tumor or took his life.

In the past when I was angry with God, I realized that I had to forgive Him just like I forgave everyone else. I had to cancel the debt that I *perceived* He owed me and let go of my expectations of Him and how I thought He should work in my life. So I did. And I did it a lot. It's not that God needs me to forgive Him, it's that I needed that "get-out-of-jail-free" card every time I was disappointed in God's performance. You see, I had God on a performance-based acceptance system where I would trust Him and be thankful when He performed to my liking. I didn't realize that I was doing that until many years after I had come to know Him.

Keeping one's accounts at zero—throwing off burdens and refusing to carry around anger and resentment—plays a huge part in finding healing and freedom in one's spiritual journey. That's what a Valley Girl or Guy learns to do if they want to survive and thrive in their valleys.

1 2

WALKING THROUGH YOUR VALLEYS

Life is like a box of chocolates. You never know what you are going to get.

—Forrest Gump

*I*t was a cloudy day in Boston, Massachusetts. I'd spent the majority of my day in our hotel room overlooking the Charles River, reading *Ruthless Trust* by Brennan Manning. What brought me to Boston? I was there with Ken who was there on business. But that's not what *really* brought me back to this city, so rich in history and higher learning. My Dad in Heaven brought me here because He had to get my undivided attention without all the existing distractions in my life at the time. He had to slow me down and quiet me down.

Ruthless trust. The words themselves paint a picture of the kind of trust God might require of us. There are several ways to define *ruthless*, but what speaks to me with a resounding clarity is the word *severe*; a trust in God that becomes extreme and intense when we are stretched and challenged. Like Manning (even mentioning his name in relation to myself seems arrogant in light of his spiritual insights and maturity), God has taught me about this kind of trust in the depths of my pain and darkness. Manning put it this way, "Through the countless hours of silence, solitude, soul-searching and prayer, I learned that the act of trust is an utterly ruthless act."

I've noticed that my hunger and deepest desire to know Jesus has only increased over the years as I've come to know Him and experience His presence in the cumulative moments of my life. It seems the more I thirst for Him, the more I know Him and also, the more I need Him. Yet, all the busyness in life is a distraction from this deep, and ever-increasing, inner desire. So, I asked my Heavenly Dad to show me ways to make time, on a regular basis, to just *be*. He answered my prayer when He brought me *back* to Boston to learn to just *be*. My grace journey began there almost exactly six years prior, when I visited the home of Henry Thoreau at Walden's Pond just outside of Boston. The words he once penned leaped out at me, "I went to the woods because I wished to live deliberately, to front only the essential facts of life, and see if I could learn what it had to teach, and not, when I come to die, discover that I had not lived." I didn't learn "the essential facts of life" that day at Walden's Pond, but I learned what they were not.

I'm a type A personality; you know, someone who is always busy, driven, on fire (or putting out fires), and running circles around the rest of humanity who get dizzy just watching this whirlwind. Perhaps that describes some of you, as well. I was a person who didn't know how to just *be*. Because of this, much of my spiritual growth has meant learning the art of *being*, which I owe to Manning.

The first step was coming to the place where I noticed that there was a problem. I had to begin making some adjustments in my lifestyle and consciously prioritizing my time to make the most out of the moments I'd been given, since busyness is the chief nemesis of all those in ministry. All the busyness and distractions that keep us from just *being* and hearing God's voice unwittingly create a lot of pain.

As a counselor, I listen to people talk about their challenges and heartaches every day and it all leads me to the same conclusion: suffering is no respecter of persons. It touches everyone's life, whether they are a Christians or not. In fact, I often think that God's kids might suffer more, which sounds crazy when I actually put that on paper or say it out loud. Why on earth would a child of God suffer more than someone who has never tasted the goodness of His love and grace? Wouldn't they suffer less? I have a theory about that.

What are the things in your life that brought you to Jesus in the first place, and what are the things since then that have produced the most growth in your life? For me, it has been the pain and struggles I've walked through. Let's face it, if everything in life was going great and we had no pain, we wouldn't need God. The pain and suffering tells me I need him and brings me to Him. I'm embarrassed to say that when I'm hurting, I read my Bible and pray more; and when things are relatively calm, I tend to be distracted by the busyness of life; my more sequestered time with the Lord becoming secondary. To be sure, I'm in prayer and connecting to the Lord throughout my day, but I really do need that undistracted time with Him when it's quiet and

YOLANDA COHEN STITH

still. But no, we tend to call on God only in emergencies even though our humanity, weaknesses, and limitations shout to us that we need Him all the time.

Since I'm a bottom-line kind of a gal, let me put it to you this way: Jesus is Life and the rest is details! My purpose on this planet is not to accomplish, achieve, build, create, birth, fix, or organize (contrary to what others may think!), and neither is yours. I wasn't *wired* to be type A. I was *wired* to be in Christ! The type A conundrum was my way of avoiding all the junk I buried that God was trying to unearth. The trouble was that it was the way I operated for so long that I didn't know how to live any other way. If I wasn't accomplishing something, then I would believe I wasn't significant or adequate. The doing and the accomplishing gave me a false sense of identity, an identity constructed from my efforts, achievements, and labor. When I was busy, I avoided the nagging emptiness that always lurked just under the surface. When I stopped and just allowed myself to *be*, I would eat to fill the void within me, food being my drug of choice. So, staying busy was a way to control the unrest inside that led to eating when I was idle. Of course, it didn't work; it only created a cycle of stress and weight gain. How many different sizes of clothes do I need to have in my closet before I recognize that something's amiss?

We live in a busy world, and Christians are some of the busiest people in the world, especially if they are in ministry. Busyness itself is like a drug. It keeps you from thinking and feeling. Busyness is the way we escape from the pain that's buried deep inside us. It could be the pain of feeling like a failure, or feeling unloved and lonely, or feeling afraid or anxious about what comes next. When I'm busy, I don't have time to think about these things.

Busyness is like an opiate that keeps me in a state of numbness. Chocolate cake can do the same thing, as a matter of fact!

God will let us run around in circles, turn cartwheels, and pull rabbits out of hats until we collapse in a heap of disillusionment and despair, or worse—become physically ill from the sheer stress and pressure of a lifestyle that would exhaust even God if that were possible!

Why? Doesn't He care? Doesn't He love us enough to save us from ourselves? Oh, yes, my dear friend, He does. He loves us enough to watch our fleshly pursuits as we justify them by calling them "ministry," because He's waiting. Our Dad is really good at waiting. Have you noticed that too? It's because He's outside of time where waiting is a non-issue. He waits until we stop, and when we've stopped, zapped of our energy to start again, He speaks. The problem is we can't hear Him speak *until* we've stopped! It's a Catch-22!

For the first time in my life, through my own counseling, I had to stop and think and feel the pain I had buried deep within; the pain of my childhood and beyond. It was there that I came to know my Dad in a completely different way, and I came to love and accept myself, not on the basis of my performance (thank you, Jesus!), but on the basis of God's sovereign grace that made me totally and completely loved and lovable! Those two little truths saved and transformed my life.

Living in the moment—right here, right now—is the only place to hear the music. Jesus is the music, but you can't hear its melody or feel its passion when you're distracted. I trust that He will wait until you've stopped, when your strength and desire to continue is gone; then you, too, will hear the music. Without the valleys in my life, the music wouldn't have the movement, clarity, or quality that I hear today in my relationship with the Lord.

STAYING IN THE MOMENT

The future. It's hard to resist the temptation to go there, isn't it? The Evil One will do everything he can to get us to camp there with the campfire blazing, stoking the logs by feeding our fear with all sorts of speculation and query. He'll even provide the marshmallows for roasting, but don't fall for it. The songs sung at this camp will not warm your heart; they will not encourage you or help you find comfort. Around this campfire, you will only find other "future" campers struggling with fear and discontent just like you are.

Living in the present requires trust. Lately, I have found trust to be a nebulous thing in the midst of my circumstances. You can't just make yourself trust. Trust is something that is produced, cultivated, and grown by the work of God's grace in the valleys of our lives. We may *want* to trust God with the future, the unknown, and the what-ifs in life; but only God can truly bring us to the place of *actual* trusting.

How do you trust God? You must know and believe at a heart level that He is a good, good Father. You must have settled the questions and false concepts you once had of Him. Dependence upon, or trust in, the Lord Jesus develops in our lives as we mature and grow through experience, *especially* our valley experiences. Experience is our teacher and the valley is the classroom. My experience as a counselor tells me that ninety percent of what we actually learn and know comes from experience, which could have a lot to do with why the educational system in this country is so inferior to many other countries based on national test scores and other measures of academic success. The majority of our academic instruction from early childhood through college finds us passively sitting in front of teachers lecturing to us, or buried under pages and pages of facts, theories, and statistics; versus engaging in experiential discovery, as in classrooms in other countries.

As I look back on the past forty years of my own life, I can see very clearly how God developed my trust in Him. While I love to read and study the Scriptures, my ability to trust Him did not grow from knowledge of God or biblical truth; it grew from experiencing God in times of great difficulty, disappointment, and crisis. That's not to say that we don't need to know what the Bible says. It's just that the Bible is the starting point but experiencing the truth of the Bible is where our transformation takes place. Through my experiences, God is developing in me a radical trust—a trust that offers no guarantees of better days, happy circumstances, or feeling good. Radical trust comes from faith and hope in the love of God through His Son, Jesus. Period. You can't learn this kind of trust just from reading a book, even the Bible, though it is indeed the inspired Word of God (Hebrews 4:12). You can learn *about* trust, but to really learn it is to know it experientially. Sorry, all you Evangelical intellectuals who think the end all is knowledge.

IT'S LOVE, NOT KNOWLEDGE

If we love God, we will trust Him. If we love Him, we will love others. It's pretty simple. I don't need a M.Div. or PhD to understand what Jesus Himself taught:

You shall love the Lord your God with all your heart, and with all your soul, and with all your mind. This is the greatest commandment. The second is like it, you shall love your neighbor as yourself. (Matthew 22:37-39)

This reminds me of something that the Lord taught me about love and trust many years ago that I've never forgotten. I love to tell this story whenever I'm speaking to a large group. It's about my relationship with my sister, which has always been on and off—mostly off—and never very close. As I've mentioned, she is thirteen years older than I and left home when I was very young.

One year, Rhoda invited my family and me to New York to spend Thanksgiving with her, which we had never done in the past. While we were alone one day, she and I were reminiscing about the family and, specifically, our parents when she noticed my earrings and asked if they were Mom's diamond earrings. My mother had always told me that she was going to give them to me, since diamonds are my birthstone. Then, when she moved from LA to Maryland where we lived, she gave them to me. When Rhoda asked me if Mom gave them to me, I told her she had. She proceeded to tell me that Mom had always told *her* that she would leave them to her. I was shocked. It was tense and awkward. I told her I had no idea and that maybe Mom got confused, since she was getting old and eventually developed dementia. Rhoda made out that she didn't care and appeared to slough it off, but I knew that, to Rhoda, it was just another confirmation of what she believed about herself and her relationship with our mother. Nothing more was said about the earrings, but I felt terrible.

The following spring, Rhoda and I were chatting on the phone and the subject of politics came up. I didn't bring it up. I have since learned to navigate away from that topic, as well as a few others, when it is brought up. The conversation went south really fast and she got angry with me because I said I didn't agree with her. Both my siblings are on opposite end from me on the political spectrum. She wanted to hang up on me, but I urged her not to and told her that I was sorry. I was always sorry when my sister became angry with me. I began to explain to her that I loved her unconditionally. She told me she didn't believe in "unconditional love" and never loved anyone that way, perhaps with the exception of her son. We managed to end the phone call in a civil manner that day, but what she said about unconditional love really stuck with me.

The following year was Ben's Bar Mitzvah and Rhoda was flying down from New York to attend, and it just so happened it was the week of her birthday. The thought came to me, *Yolanda, give your sister your Mother's diamond earrings for her birthday.* It was the Lord speaking to me and I was so excited. I knew that those earrings would be the perfect demonstration of unconditional love. I found a little velvet box and placed the earrings in it and placed it in a pretty little gift bag. When my sister arrived, I gave her the present, and she opened the velvet box and knew immediately they were Mom's earrings. She started to become emotional, but in typical Rhoda fashion, she held back her tears and put on a stoic front, not allowing herself to appear vulnerable. To this day, I don't know the impact of that gift on her, but I've never had more joy in giving something to someone as I did those earrings to my beloved sister. My hope and prayer for her is that one day she too will experience the kind of love that I have from God—just because, unconditional, unearned, and freely given.

Trusting God that loving and giving to my sister would have an eternal reward for her and for me has been my focus, but it hasn't been easy. Old wounds continue to reopen exposing the years of hurt. Many times, I've caught myself trying to earn her love and acceptance in an effort to have that sister-relationship which has eluded me for most of my life. When someone has expectations of you and looks to you and others to make them feel loved, secure, and valued, the relationship is going to be difficult, because those things come from within and not without. In typical fashion, my sister would get angry with me about something I'd said or done and confront me with how I messed up or withdraw from me altogether. Those times of withdrawal can stretch into years. This has been a painful valley where I must accept that this relationship may never be what I would like it to be, which I may never understand. All I know is I am not her Source. I am just a resource for God to use in her life, but she doesn't have faith or a relationship with the Living God, so she's made me (and others) her Source.

Radical trust endures even when understanding fails. God moves us from trust in an experience of God, to the love of God, to faith and hope in God. This is what produces trust. It doesn't mean we won't struggle with doubt or fear. How can we experience faith if we've never doubted, or hope if we've never been in despair?

No matter where we are on the journey to know, through our experience, the reality of life in Jesus, we can and will learn that God's love for us endures every evil and the pain and loss that result from it. God's love endures our every weakness and our every failure. "We know it so well, we've embraced it heart and soul, *this love that comes from God*" (1 John 4:16, MSG).

I have experienced the love of God through those who have walked with me in my valleys, in the most difficult and painful seasons in my life. The prayers and words of encouragement during my dark nights of the soul have served as beacons of God's love for me when, on my own, that light would have easily been extinguished. In the valleys, God provides a way, a hope, and a light to keep us moving forward and to show us His faithfulness, which gives birth to our trust.

MAN'S BASIC PROBLEM: OUR PERCEIVED NEED TO CONTROL

As we move through the twists and turns of valley life, God continues to deal with our never-ending perceived need to control. I can tell you firsthand, it just doesn't work in the valley. You never really know just how much you like to be in control until that control is taken away. The truth is, we never really are in control; it's just an illusion. There are specific things in daily living over which we like to have control, like having quiet time and choosing what we want to do on our days off from work, for instance. Certainly, our world is not going to come to an end if we can't have what we want when we want it, but when we're used to having a certain amount of perceived control, it's annoying when it's gone!

We all like to think that we're not one of those controlling types. We are quick to judge and condemn others as having "control issues," but when it comes to ourselves, we seem to be shortsighted. The truth of the matter is that we all have "control issues," a perceived need to control ourselves, others (including God), and circumstances to maintain a sense of security and wellbeing. This need to control becomes the primary way in which we try to get our needs met and, perhaps unwittingly, build an identity apart from God. In fact, this perceived need to control is the result of what happened in the Garden.

I tend to forget that I really need to depend on Jesus for *all things*, not just for the crisis situations. The life God wants for me is beyond what I can manage on my own. I tend to avoid the things in my life that I know I can't handle. I think a lot of us do. They scare me and make me feel insecure, so I try to create a world for myself where I feel like I am in control, even if it's only an illusion. When my house is clean and things are put away where they belong and the bed is made exactly the way I like—with hospital corners like Sergeant Cohen taught me—I feel a sense of security and well-being and believe I am in control! There are times when I can orchestrate this false sense of security, but real security only comes from Christ and God wants to remind me of that in tangible ways.

There are times when my perceived need to control and manage things really shocks me and makes me wonder what the heck I was thinking? During the time we lived in England, I got involved with an organization on the air base called Protestant Women of the Chapel (PWOC) as their spiritual director. I chose and led all the Bible studies and provided spiritual guidance for all the women in the organization. Every two years, PWOC would elect new officers to fill the positions of president, vice president, and secretary. Once elected, the new president would appoint the spiritual director. During my tenure, our studies encouraged and fostered spiritual growth and insights into the Old Testament and our Jewish spiritual roots. This was years before the "wheels fell of my bus" and to say that I thought of myself as having arrived would indeed be accurate. Even with all the members of PWOC coming from different church backgrounds, they were all receptive to my leadership, probably because I'm a natural salesperson!

It came time for the bi-annual elections. Nominations

were taken for each position. The current president was my best friend. It was she who had appointed me as the spiritual director. One of the nominations for the new president was someone that neither of us had a fondness for (the Christian way of saying we didn't like her!). Her leadership style would be very legalistic. I could not bear to see our group head off course into that direction. When all the ballots were placed in the voting box, the Evil One whispered to me, *Just take her name out of the box and she won't be elected.* At that time, I don't think I even recognized where that evil thought came from. Instead, I was convinced this was the right thing to do, thinking the end would justify the means. When I think of this now, I can clearly see my need to control. My level of trusting God back in those days needed some serious attention.

When I told my friend, the out-going president, what I was going to do, she quickly brought me to my senses. I really needed that "come to Jesus" moment. Thankfully, I accepted her counsel and, yes, the woman in question became our new president. If we would stop and think about all the ways we employ our control tactics to achieve our desired outcomes, it's staggering. We justify and make excuses, but the bottom line is we aren't trusting God.

My grace is sufficient for you, for power is perfected in weakness. Most gladly, therefore, I will rather boast about my weaknesses, that the power of Christ may dwell in me. Therefore, I am well content with weaknesses, with insults, with distresses, with persecutions, with difficulties, for Christ's sake; for when I am weak, then I am strong. (2 Corinthians 12:9-10)

THE WHITE FLAG OF SURRENDER

There is no way to thrive in the Christian life, much less conquer the desolate valleys, without coming to a place of giving up; which, mind you, is not the same thing as giving in. When Rachel was young and didn't want to get in trouble with her mom, she would "give in" and comply with me outwardly, but on the inside she was as determined as ever to have her way. Real surrender, as opposed to offering a semblance of surrender, means truly yielding to someone.

I don't always see things God's way and He rarely shares His perspective with me. I prefer the road of least resistance, avoiding pitfalls and discomfort, but He doesn't exactly oblige me. Somewhere along the line I realized that God and I have a different goal. His goal is my personal growth and my goal is my happiness. Things like pain and suffering, conflict, set-backs, and disappointments are all things He uses to develop and grow my faith.

How do you know when you need to surrender something or someone to God? It's pretty simple. You know the moment you realize you've shifted from resting in God to struggling. Remember, the reason we begin to struggle is because we are trying to maintain control and that persistent controlling is the vehicle we use to try to meet our God-given needs through our own resources.

Here's an example. I'm on the Beltway and I need to get to my destination in thirty minutes to make an appointment with someone on time, but the Beltway is like a parking lot in the middle of the day. I'm beginning to get upset. I start driving a little recklessly, weaving in and out of lanes and fuming at the driver in front of me. My emotions climb the emotional Richter scale from the point of resting and calm to frustration and full-blown anger. I need to surrender the situation to the Lord. But there are a couple of things at play that I need to become aware of first. One, I need to understand why I'm so upset. Two, I need to determine the need (which is linked to my identity) that I believe is not being met in that moment. You see, what I need to surrender is getting my need met my own way instead of through trusting Christ. In this scenario, what got me worked up is that I am going to be late and I don't like being late. I'm almost never late. Why? Because I learned at a young age that when you are late and keep people waiting, they will not be happy with you. Unfortunately, I have a deep-rooted and erroneous belief that I need people to be happy with me in order to be okay. While it may very well be a belief, is it true? No, absolutely not. And what need am I trying to meet through making people happy with me? At least one of three: love, security, or significance. I would say its love and security, because when people are unhappy with me, I feel unloved and insecure. Easy, right? Who is the only one who can meet my need for love and security? God, of course! So this is one of a million examples I could use of wresting control of my circumstances or people in an effort to meet needs that only God can meet. The only viable way out is to surrender the situation and my need for love and security to Jesus. In order to do this, however, I must be willing to experience things that I'm trying really hard to avoid, like feeling unloved and insecure which might or might not be the end result of my late arrival. In reality, while I may not like it; even *if* the person waiting is angry and frustrated with me, my identity (my being okay) is not contingent upon what others think or do. Once I recognize the lie that I've believed, I can choose the truth and surrender my arrival time to God. I must be willing to be late and trust the Lord with the outcome. Guess what happens every time I choose to surrender the situation to the Lord? The person I'm meeting with cancels, is tied up with something else, or isn't there at all because he was stuck in traffic!

Surrender is trusting God with both our outcomes and getting our needs met. The more I grow in my understanding of my identity and walk in it, the less I worry about what others think of me, but instead place my confidence in Christ. When my clients are struggling, I don't even have to ask if they are practicing surrender, because I know they aren't.

Some of our pain is the result of challenging circumstances or things others do that affect us, but some of our pain and suffering is self-inflicted simply because we believe things that aren't true and that leads us to the struggle.

Walking through your valleys and experiencing the pain and suffering in those valleys is your opportunity for growing in Christ. It is a matter of learning to *be* and developing an intimacy with the living God and at the same time letting go of your ways of controlling your life, so that you can embrace the God who is in control of all things, both positive and negative.

Yes, giving up control is always going to be challenging for us because of what happened in the Garden. Remember the movie, *Bruce Almighty*? Jim Carey plays a self-centered, obsessively compulsive, and ambitious news reporter for a local television station. On this particular day, it seems as though everything that could go wrong does go wrong. In a moment of desperation, Bruce prays that God would give him a break. Well, God does better than that, he allows him to be God. At first, he enjoys the power and freedom to orchestrate events and affect people's lives, but before long he discovers that being God is not all it's cracked up to be. At the end of the movie, when his life is a mess, and he's come to the end of himself, he cries out to God, "I give up! I don't want to be God anymore. I don't want to decide what's right or what's wrong. I surrender to your will." This is the place where we must all eventually come. I don't know if I'm there yet, but I am closer today than I was last week!

VALLEY LIFE

I don't mind saying that I'm a Valley Girl. The valley is where I cut my spiritual teeth as a follower of Jesus. Every lesson of any value I've learned has been learned there and I'm not alone. Every spiritual giant in the Bible, every great theologian, and all the nameless men and women who have been martyred for their faith have spent significant amounts of time in the valley. And I'm grateful for a God who, while leading us to *"the valley of the shadow of death,"* doesn't abandon us there. As a result of the cross, God is not only with us He is in us and we are in Him; therefore, there is nothing too dark or too painful that we cannot endure by His grace.

It's not on the mountaintops that you grow your spiritual muscles; it's in the dark, lonely valleys of your life. That's where you hear the beautiful music playing. There, in your silent moments where the light of God's grace and goodness shines most brightly. He's there; and, while all other gods fail us, He is enough.

Whatever valley you're entering, leaving, or currently in, my prayer is that you will savor the truths that you learn from being there. This is not a place of punishment, but a place of higher learning. Even though it's human nature to run from pain and suffering, there is, in the valley, a storehouse of immeasurable wealth, a treasure too great to place a value on, and a wisdom that far exceeds the greatest scholastic achievements ever written by man.

THE END

ABOUT THE AUTHOR

Yolanda Cohen Stith is a Christian pastoral counselor and has been in ministry since 1997. She and her late husband cofounded a Christ-centered counseling and teaching ministry in the Washington, DC, area. She has a blog on the New Heart Living Facebook page, where she shares biblical truths, often in the context of her own life experiences.

Writing is one of Yolanda's passions. She has written curriculum for classes used at New Heart Living and other counseling offices. Her writing includes a lot of humor and wit that is both vulnerable and personal.

Yolanda has gone through extensive training through Network 220 (teaching Christians their identity in Christ and the full implications of the cross) and is commissioned through that organization. Her message is biblically sound as she seeks to challenge the body of Christ and expose faulty teaching within the church.

She often speaks at women's church retreats and Fourth-Day community retreats.

To learn more about Yolanda or book her to speak at an event, visit: **www.yolandacohenstith.com**